WILLIAMSBURG RESEARCH STUDIES

D1177978

Criminal Trial Proceedings
in the General Court
of Colonial Virginia

Criminal Trial Proceedings in the General Court of Colonial Virginia

By

HUGH F. RANKIN

Justice is a machine that, when some one has once given it the starting push, rolls on of itself.

JOHN GALSWORTHY, *Justice.*

COLONIAL WILLIAMSBURG

Williamsburg, Virginia

Distributed by

THE UNIVERSITY PRESS OF VIRGINIA

Charlottesville

FOREWORD

WILLIAMSBURG RESEARCH STUDIES is a series of
specialized reports prepared in the research program of
Colonial Williamsburg. For almost forty years this program has sought to fulfill a dual objective: to supply
the day-to-day information essential to the accurate pre-
servation and restoration of Virginia's colonial capital,
and to supplement the interpretation of Williamsburg with
studies broader in scope but as detailed in content. The
series will make available in inexpensive form those studies
of widest interest to students of the era and locality.

To inaugurate the series, we have chosen seven
reports from the files of the Research Department. These
studies originally were for internal use only; some are
largely compilations of the documentary sources relating
to a subject, and others are more interpretive. Future
titles will appear as research projects are concluded and
will include contributions from the fields of architecture,
archaeology, hand crafts, and the decorative arts.

For permission to publish certain copyrighted
material in this volume, we should like to express apprecia-
tion to the Henry E. Huntington Library and Art Gallery,

San Marino, California; and the Virginia Historical Society
and the Virginia State Library, Richmond, Virginia. Trans-
cripts of Crown copyright material in the Public Record
Office, London, appear by permission of the Controller
of Her Majesty's Stationery Office. Chapters II and III
appeared originally in the <u>Virginia Magazine of History
and Biography</u>, LXX (1960), 142-153, and LXXII (1964), 50-
74, and are reprinted by permission of the editor.

Edward M. Riley
Director of Research

CONTENTS

Criminal Trial Proceedings in the General Court of Colonial Virginia

Chapter I

THE DEVELOPMENT OF THE GENERAL COURT

Among the frailties of man is that trait which allows him to return to a state of nature when not under restrictions applied by some higher authority. This weakness becomes particularly apparent when transplanting people overseas, and in almost one motion snatching them from all of the adornments of a civilized society and setting them down in a raw wilderness.

The first court of Virginia, out of which was to evolve the superior court of that colony, arose out of the recognition of such a need of regulation. The judicial system of England, well established and smoothly operating though it might be, could not be transported into the environment of Jamestown and be expected to fit the needs of the colonials. And it was an awareness of unknown factors that possibly accounts for the vagueness and indecision in those early instructions that were to become the basis for the court structure of colonial Virginia.

The first charter of Virginia, dated April 10, 1606, decreed that the colony should have a council of thirteen persons, "which shall govern and order all Matters and Causes which shall arise...."[1] On November 20, 1606, clarifying "Articles, Instructions and Orders" were issued, listing those crimes punishable by death and "that the said several presidents and councells, and the greater number of them...shall have full power and authority, to hear and determine all and every the offences aforesaid...." In addition, there were provisions for a jury trial with twelve jurors in all felonies. Civil cases likewise fell within the jurisdiction of the President and Council whose authority was extended to sentencing offenders to a "reasonable corporal punishment and imprisonment, or else by a convenient fine, awarding damages or other satisfaction, to the party grieved...." Misdemeanors were to be adjudged "accoring to their best

---

1. William Stith, The History of the First Discovery and Settlement of Virginia: Being an Essay Towards a General History of this Colony (Williamsburg, 1747), appendix, p. 3; William Waller Hening, ed., The Statutes at Large: Being a Collection of all the Laws of Virginia from the First Session of the Legislature, in the Year 1619 (New York, 1810-1823), I, 63.

discretions, and with such convenient punishment, as they or the most part of them shall think fitt."[2]

And so it was that at this early date the Council, primarily intended as a governing body, was also extended a judicial function. Other than the duties outlined in the charter, there was never a commission issued the Council as a court, nor did they ever take the accepted oath of a judge. Out of such haphazard beginnings rose an unique political institution, a body involved in the formulating of policy as the upper house of the Assembly and in interpreting this policy as the highest court of the colony.[3]

When the Virginia Company was issued a new charter, May 23, 1609, there was still the vagueness with respect to courts and judicature that had characterized the original document. The primary jurisdiction still rested with the Council "within the said Precincts of Virginia, or in the Way by Sea thither and from thence,

_____

2. Hening, Statutes, I, 69-71.

3. Henry Hartwell, James Blair and Edward Chilton, The Present State of Virginia and the College, ed. by Hunter Dickinson Farish (Williamsburg, 1940), p. 47. The original date of this publication was 1700.

have full and absolute power and authority, to correct,
punish, pardon, govern and rule...at any time hereafter...."
This same month, however, saw the issuance of new "Instruc-
cions Orders and Constititucions," to Sir Thomas Gates,
Governor of Virginia, which, in effect, voided the provisions of the second charter in that Gates was empowered
to initiate martial law if deemed necessary to rectify
the "misery and misgovernment" then so prevalent in
Jamestown.[4]

This temporary dictatorship continued through
Gates' successor, Sir Thomas Dale, whose forbidding title
of "Marshal" suggests more the despot than the judge.
The third charter of the Virginia Company, of March 12,
1612, was equally obscure in delineating the judicial
functions of the Council and merely confirmed former

---

4. Stith, <u>History of the First Discovery and Settle-
ment of Virginia</u>, appendix, p. 20; Alexander Brown, <u>The
Genesis of the United States: A Narrative of the Movement
in England, 1605-1616, Which Resulted in the Plantation
of North America by Englishmen, Disclosing the Contest
Between England and Spain for the Possession of the Soil
Now Occupied by the United States of America: Set Forth
Through a Series of Historical Documents now First Printed</u>,
<u>Together with a Reissue of Rare Contemporaneous Tracts</u>,
<u>Accompanied by Bibliographical Memoranda, Notes and Brief
Biographies</u> (Boston, 1890), I, 301; Hening, <u>Statutes</u>, I,
96; Susan Myra Kingsbury, ed., <u>The Records of the Virginia
Company of London</u> (Washington, 1906-1935), III, 15;

privileges. There were, however, additional provisions

for those who had deserted the colony. They were to be

either punished in England or returned to Virginia, "there

to be proceeded against and punished, as the governor,

deputy, or council there,...shall think meet; or other-

wise according to such laws and ordinances, as are and

shall be in use there, for the well-ordering and good

government of the said colony." Actually, it was not

until 1622 that the Council of the Virginia Company was

able to report that "The rigour of Martiall Law, where-

with before they were governed, is reduced within the

limits prescribed by his Majesty: and the Laudable forme

of Justice and government used in this Realm, established,

and followed as neere as may be."[5]

The Quarter Court, the precursor of the General

Court, was provided for in the "Instructions to the Gov-

ernor and Council of State in Virginia," issued by the

Alexander Brown, The First Republic in America: An Account
of the Origins of this Nation, Written from the Records
then (1624) Concealed by the Council, Rather than from
the Histories then Licensed by the Crown (Boston, 1898),
p. 117.

5. Kingsbury, Records of the Virginia Company, III,
26, 310; Hening, Statutes, I, 98-110; Stith, History of
the First Discovery and Settlement of Virginia, appendix,
pp. 23-32.

Virginia Company to George Yeardley, July 24, 1621. The
Governor and Council were directed to "sett doune the
fittest months" for the quarterly meeting with considera-
tion for "the best ease and benefit of the people that
shall have occasion to address themselves unto the Council wither for Justice or direction...." The governor
still held powers to punish "contempt of authority in
any kind," and in certain instances was empowered to
summon a council extraordinary to examine a case of a
recalcitrant councillor.[6] In this latter provision lay
the seed for courts of oyer and terminer.

There were those who, in seeking justification
for the dissolution of the Virginia Company through a
"Statement Touching the Miserable Condition of Virginia,"
included charges that the courts were mismanaged. But
in the subsequent commission issued to Sir Francis Wyatt

---

6. Kingsbury, Records of the Virginia Company, III,
478-480; Hening, Statutes, I, 116, 117. Because of word-
ing in instructions to Governor Nathaniel Butler of Bermuda
in 1619, "to effect reforms duplicating many of those the
preceding year for Virginia," Wesley Frank Craven feels
that instructions were issued in 1618 for the sitting of
the Governor and Council as a Quarter Court in Jamestown.
(Wesley Frank Craven, The Southern Colonies in the Seventeenth Century [Baton Rouge, 1949], pp. 133-134.) Brown
says that Yeardley had initiated monthly courts under the
civil law ordinance of 1618. (Brown, First Republic, p. 456.)

as the first royal governor of the colony, there was a
phrase continuing the judicial function of the Governor
and Council as in the past and delegating to that body
the authority "to direct and govern correct and punish
our subjects...in Virginia...."[7]

There are extant records showing that the
Council sat as a court as early as February 1622, dispensing justice in both civil and criminal cases, regulating strong drink and administering the oath of
allegiance to new arrivals in the colony. There appears
to have been no particular quorum required for judges
during this period, for it was not unknown that only
one councillor sat with the governor and, upon at least
one occasion, the governor sat alone as a court. During these early days the court customarily met at
Jamestown, but it sometimes met in other areas; as
early as 1628 it was held at Elizabeth City. There
was one rather unusual case in 1630. When Dr. John
Pott, a former governor, was found guilty of cattle-
stealing the entire Council acted as his security and

---

7. Kingsbury, Records of the Virginia Company, IV,
177, 503.

judgment was suspended until "the king's pleasure [be] known."[8]

As the colony expanded, so did the jurisdiction of the Quarter Court. Not only did they dispense justice, but they assumed some duties of a regulatory nature. By 1632 they were receiving from the clergy or churchwardens of every parish a register of christenings, marriages and burials, along with accounts of the levies, collections and disbursements of the church. They controlled the number and quality of tobacco plants, along with all Indian relations. Courts were to assemble the first of March, June, October and December, and this "public service" was considered so important that in 1626 absentee judges were fined 300 pounds of tobacco unless their excuses found favor with the governor and other judges.[9]

During the Puritan Interregnum there was a decline in the authority of the Quarter Courts, perhaps

---

8. H. R. McIlwaine, ed., Minutes of the Council and General Court of Colonial Virginia, 1622-1632, 1670-1671, with Notes and Excerpts from Original Council and General Court Records, into 1683, Now Lost (Richmond, 1924), pp. 1-12, 12-80, 185-186; Hening, Statutes, I, 145-146.

9. Hening, Statutes, I, 155, 164, 165, 167, 174, 180, 187, 189; McIlwaine, Minutes of the General Court, p. 106.

because of the general trend towards levelling during that period. County courts, established for the "punishing of petty offences," had been erected in Virginia under a statute of 1624, and were denied jurisdiction over crimes whose punishments involved the loss of life or limb. This restriction seems to have been abandoned during the Interregnum, apparently following the precedent of the quarter sessions of the English county where felonies were tried before the inferior courts. The Assembly, however, in 1656 returned such jurisdiction to the Quarter Court with the explanation:

> Wee conceive it no ease nor benefit to the
> people to have their lives taken away with
> too much ease, And though we confess the
> same to be done in England, yet wee know
> the disparity between them and us to be so
> great that wee cannot with safety follow
> the example.[10]

Although the court did travel from time to time, its regular seat was in Jamestown, and from 1643 on, it was provided quarters in the new statehouse. After the building was destroyed by fire in 1656, space for the court was rented in the tavern of Thomas Woodhouse. Such surroundings were not considered

---

10. Hening, Statutes, I, 125, 397-398.

compatible with the dignity and decorum of the court, ofttimes disturbed "by the clamorous unmannerlyness of the people." It seems that the indecorous surroundings were at least partially responsible for the demand for a new statehouse in 1663. The present quarters were not only inadequate, it was argued, but there was also "the dishonour of all our laws being made and our judgments given in alehouses."[11]

That the judicial system did not always function properly is attested by a resolution of the Assembly in March, 1658, suggesting the avoidance of too hasty adjournments of both the Quarter and the county courts, and urging "that all possible dispatch...of all causes bee made." New responsibilities were assigned the court by the Assembly. Each county sheriff, at the expiration of his one year term, was required to render his accounts at the March sitting of the court. Deserted lands (not cultivated within a three year period) had to be so declared by the court before the acreage could be regranted. It was through such a gradual enlargement of its duties

---

11. Philip Alexander Bruce, Institutional History of Virginia in the Seventeenth Century (New York, 1910), I, 653-655; Hening, Statutes, I, 425, II, 58, 204.

that the Quarter Court became an indispensable segment of the colony's government.[12]

Notwithstanding the enlarged jurisdiction of the Quarter Court, its periodic meetings were decreased in March, 1659. The June court was "totally abolished & void," with the dates for the other three meetings set for the twentieth of March, September and November. Later the March meeting was moved to April fifteenth. Although the warm weather may have been a factor, the more practical reason for cancelling the June court was, "the shipps are then out of the country, time of payment past and the crop then cheifly in hand."[13]

The term "Quarter Court" was felt to be a misnomer by 1662, and it was directed that henceforth the high court be designated the "General Court." It also became necessary to provide some protection for persons travelling to Jamestown for either the Assembly or in connection with the proceedings of the court. It had become the custom, because of the "malice of some

---

12. Hening, Statutes, I, 436, 498, 526.

13. Ibid., I, 524, II, 58, 227. The term "Quarter Court" seems to have been difficult to eliminate from everyday usage, for in 1663 the Assembly was referring to the General Court as such. (Ibid., 204.)

persons," to seize upon this opportunity to demand the arrest of those persons involved in litigation. Because of this possibility, so many persons had remained away from the capital that in 1664 it was felt necessary to prohibit, by statute, the arrest of any visitor not a citizen of James City County (unless a felony was involved) five days before and five days after the meeting of the court.[14]

From 1666, the year of the completion of the second statehouse, to 1676 when it was burned, sessions of the General Court were conducted in that building. When the Capitol was put to the torch by Nathaniel Bacon and his followers, the court became something of an ambulatory body, first meeting in the home of Colonel William Browne. After the court and Assembly both began to meet in the house of a Mrs. Macon, Captain William Armiger was remunerated for supplying a picture of the king's arms, a chair and other furnishings for the use of both groups. After the burning of the third statehouse at Jamestown, the court met in a Mr. Sherwood's

---

14. Hening, Statutes, II, 58, 204, 213.

Great Hall until its eventual removal to Williamsburg.[15]

To enable the governor and his councillors to understand the intricacies of the law, a levy was laid upon tobacco to provide funds with which to purchase all English statutes printed prior to 1666, along with Michael Dalton's Justice of the Peace and Swinburne's Wills and Testaments. It would seem, from Thomas Ludwell's laudatory report of 1666, that the court had already made use of such guides, for it was his opinion that

> greate care is taken to make the Lawes and
> pleadings upon them easy & obvious to any
> mans und'standing as in other parts they doe
> keep them a mystery to the people for noe
> advantage is allowed to either party from
> little errors in Declarations or Pleas &c.[16]

As a result of the turmoil generated by Bacon's rebellion, all courts of adjudication were "shutt up," and in February, 1677, it was felt necessary to pass an act re-opening the courts as soon as possible "that justice may againe bee freely exercised and done in all causes where it shall be required." Governor William

---

15. Bruce, Institutional History of Virginia in the Seventeenth Century, I, 653-655; Hening, Statutes, I, 425.

16. Hening, Statutes, II, 246; Thomas Ludwell, "A Description of the Government of Virginia," Virginia Magazine of History and Biography, V (July, 1897), 57.

Berkeley, eager to try for treason those who had disrupted his government, was not lax in dispensing his
ideas of justice. Assembling the Council at Green Spring,
he instituted proceedings akin to courts martial, although
there was some semblance of civil authority in that the
accused were tried by jury.[17]

The instructions issued to Governor Lord Thomas
Culpeper in 1682 contained the directive "to erect constitute and establish...Courts of Judicature" with the
advice of Council, itself a suggestion that the courts
of the colony, since the end of the rebellion, had been
functioning poorly and were in need of reorganization.
It would seem, from the later analysis of Robert Beverley,
that the courts were more concerned with the "Nicety of
Pleasing" in their judgments, while the clerks, in recording, were so entering judgments as to make them inflexible
precedents for the future. Culpeper arrived in the colony
during the plant cutters' trials and "thought fit to mingle
mercy with justice," mollifying charges of treason with
humane insight. The governor examined the General Court
proceedings and not only streamlined them, but also the

17. Hening, Statutes, II, 401, 422.

methods of recording judgments, apparently feeling

that the local courts were not yet experienced enough

"to be able to make Precedents for Posterity," and

judgments could not always be just if warped and bound

by past decisions.[18]

Among other judicial reforms executed during

Culpeper's administration was a reduction of the Gen-

eral Court to two sessions a year rather than the pre-

vious three. It was held that the former meetings in

September were "too early before tobacco comes in de-

mand and ships arrivall into this country," while the

near winter weather in November exposed both judges and

litigants to "great hazard and detriment." With this

in mind, the new dates for the sitting of the court were

April and October fifteenth (unless these days fell on

a Sunday), and were to continue for eighteen days

---

18. "Virginia in 1682," Virginia Magazine of History
and Biography, XXVI (July, 1918), 260; Robert Beverley,
The History and Present State of Virginia, ed. by Louis B.
Wright (Chapel Hill, 1947), pp. 94-95; H. R. McIlwaine and
Wilmer L. Hall, eds., Executive Journals of the Council of
Colonial Virginia (Richmond, 1925-1945), I, 492-493;
Virginia Magazine of History and Biography, XXIII (April,
1915), 147; Culpeper to the Lords of Trade, September 20,
1683, PRO CO5/1356, Virginia Colonial Records Project
microfilm, Colonial Williamsburg, Inc.

thereafter, excluding the Sabbath.[19]

This same session of April, 1684, saw the Assembly laying a levy upon all spiritous liquors for the construction of a new statehouse to house the legislature and the General Court. Although the curtailment of the sittings of the court met with the approbation of the crown, a clause was inserted by the home government, delegating to the governor the "power of appointing Courts to be held att any time whatever...."[20]

In 1691 when Francis Nicholson arrived in Virginia as lieutenant-governor and as presiding officer of the General Court he adhered strictly to the letter of the law. No deviations were tolerated and the statutes of the colony governed his judgments "where-ever they happen'd not to be silent." Conversely, when he was succeeded by Sir Edmund Andros in 1692, the new governor based his decisions upon the statutes of England, and even English custom and usage, whether or

---

19. Hening, Statutes, III, 10-11.

20. Ibid., III, 23; H. R. McIlwaine, ed., Legislative Journals of the Council of Colonial Virginia (Richmond, 1918-1919), I, 84.

not it was applicable to the colony.[21] This variance

was, to say the least, confusing, and by 1698 one writer

penned a rather caustic censure of Virginia judicial

procedures. Not among the least misfortunes, he said,

was that

> it is not clear what is the law whereby they
> are governed. They all agree in this, that
> the two fountains of their law are the laws
> of England, and the acts of their own general
> assemblies; but how far both, or either of
> these is to take place, is in the judge's
> heart, and is applied according to their
> particular affection to the party.[22]

Following the destruction by fire of the third

statehouse in Jamestown and the Assembly's decision to

move the capital to Middle Plantation, the Council ordered

the attorney-general to prepare and issue a proclamation

that after May 10, 1700, all General Courts were to sit

at Williamsburg. At the conclusion of the April court,

however, and apparently no end in sight to the construc-

tion of the new Capitol, the court adjourned until

---

21. Beverley, History and Present State of Virginia, pp. 94-95.

22. "An Account of the Present State and Government of Virginia," Collections of the Massachusetts Historical Society for the Year M, DCC, XCVIII, 1st series, V (Boston, 1798), 146-149.

October, but not until after they had accepted the hospitality extended by the Trustees of the College of William and Mary inviting them to use the college facilities. By the middle of July, it was evident that the new capital city could not provide accommodations for both the Assembly and the General Court; thereupon the Assembly was prorogued until late October.[23]

The construction of the new Capitol met with one delay after the other. The committee appointed to revise the laws had been designated to oversee the building program. Yet when that committee's term expired in 1703, the building was still unfinished and a joint committee of the House of Burgesses and the Council were named to supervise the completion of construction. As late as April, 1702, Governor Nicholson (now serving his second term) heard that the court would be sitting in the new building by October, but there was further postponement because of changes in the General Court chamber ordered by the House. These included three galleries to be constructed around the room, with specific directions for placing the chairs and benches, and

---

23. Exec. Jour. Council Col. Va., II, 14, 61, 97-98.

that the queen's arms be placed on the wall above the chair of the presiding officer. Despite these last minute alterations, the court sat in the new building for the first time in April, 1703, but apparently in unfinished quarters. In addition there was a rumor, spread by mariner Walter Cock of Surry County, that he had been told in London that a halt had been ordered in the construction of the new Capitol and that henceforth the General Court was to meet in Jamestown as formerly.[24]

The Capitol was still not complete in October, 1704, when John Page's old house, standing in the middle of Duke of Gloucester Street was demolished so as not to impair the vista from the Capitol to the college. And there were still the countless bits of minutiae that had to be done before the building could be considered complete; erecting a wall around the Capitol, securing the queen's arms and portrait for the court room and ordering the law books considered necessary for consultation by the judges.

---

24. H. R. McIlwaine, ed., Journals of the House of Burgesses in Virginia, 1695-1702 (Richmond,1906-1915),pp.177-178 [hereafter cited as JHB plus date]; Exec. Jour. Council Col. Va., II, 1-2, 323; JHB 1702-1712, pp. 29, 34; Nicholson to the Board of Trade, July 29, 1702, PRO CO5/1360 and Edmund Jenings to Lords of Plantations, July 6, 1703, PRO CO5/1313, Va. Col. Rec. microfilm.

The General Court, or rather Governor
Nicholson's conduct as presiding officer of that body,
became one of the focal points of an attempt by the
Virginians to oust the governor between 1703 and 1705.
Certainly Nicholson's behavior was not very circumspect.
Upon one occasion he siezed the attorney-general of the
colony by the collar, swearing "That he knew of no Laws
they had, and that his Commands should be obey'd without
Hesitation or Reserve." And in answer to the criticism
of some Virginians, it is reported that he dismissed
their complaints with the charge that "they were Dogs,
and their Wives were Bitches...." As for any rights
they might claim, he declared that "they had no Right
at all to the Liberties of English Subjects, and that
he wou'd hang up those that should presume to oppose
him, with Magna Charta about their Necks." When Philip
Ludwell, complaining of ill health, objected to the court
staying in session until odd hours at night, Nicholson
threatened to remove him from the Council, "and then let
me get in again How I could and be damned." In addition
to keeping the court sitting until unreasonable hours,
the list of charges against the governor included bul-
lying witnesses, packing juries, directing clerks to

change judgments already on the books, threatening

lawyers and throwing his less influential critics into

gaol without formal charges.[25]

This antipathy towards the governor and his

alleged arbitrary conduct in the General Court may well

have prompted the committee for the revisal of the laws

to attempt to alter the court in 1703. The bill, as

originally drawn, apparently was designed to lessen the

governor's judicial power through the elimination of the

executive and the Council as judges of the high court

and the appointment of five judges with prescribed terms

and qualifications. This change, after study by the

Board of Trade in London, was stricken when that agency

insisted that the Governor and Council continue as judges,

---

25. Exec. Jour. Council Col. Va., II, 365-366;
Legis. Jour. Council Col. Va., III, 1543; JHB 1702-1712,
pp. 55, 73, 75, 101-102; Philip Ludwell to James Blair,
October 21, 1702, PRO CO5/1314, Va. Col. Rec. microfilm;
JHB 1695-1702, pp. 136-137; "Charges Against Governor
Nicholson," Virginia Magazine of History and Biography,
III (April, 1896), 374, 375, 378-379; Clyde McCulloch, ed.,
"The Fight to Depose Governor Nicholson--James Blair's
Affidavit of June 7, 1704," Journal of Southern History,
XII (July, 1946), 414-422; Philip Ludwell, Stephen Fouace
and James Blair to ------, January 9, 1705, PRO CO5/1314;
[Stephen] Fouace to the Archbishop of Canterbury, Septem-
ber 28, 1702, Fulham Palace Papers 14, Va. Col. Rec.
microfilm; Beverley, History and Present State of Virginia,
pp. 106-107. At the time of his writing his Present State

with the executive and any five councillors constituting
a quorum.   There had likewise been a move to add an
additional court in December, a suggestion that was
looked upon with disfavor because at that season the
weather "rendred it abundantly more troublesome than useful." But the amount at stake in civil suits before the
General Court was increased to discourage "triviall and
small cases" that had so often consumed time in the past.[26]

There seems to have been a practical purpose
behind the proposal for an additional sitting of the
General Court, notwithstanding those inconveniences it
may have brought about. Criminals incarcerated in the
public gaol were sometimes allowed to languish for as
long as six months in conditions less than desirable.
Certainly the situation seems to have been taken cogni-
zance of by the Board of Trade, for they protested a
clause in the General Court Act of 1705 that declared
the General Court and the county courts to be the only

---

of Virginia, Beverley was harboring a grudge against Governor Nicholson for moving the capital from Jamestown and
his criticism must, to say the least, be taken with a
grain of salt. (Ibid., p. xxix.)

26. Exec. Jour. Council Col. Va., III, 106-107;
Hening, Statutes, III, 287-302.

courts of record within the colony. To the Board of

Trade, this declaration appeared to rule out courts of

oyer and terminer which might be called to relieve ac-

cused felons suffering long imprisonments. In March,

1707, they informed the Governor and Council that the

original statement would certainly meet with the dis-

approval of the crown unless a proviso was added stating,

> that nothing Contained in this Act shall be
> Construed or Deemed to Derogate from the
> Royal Power and Prerogative of her Majesty,
> her heirs, and successors of Receiving
> appeals; and of granting Commissions of Oyer
> and Terminer, or of Constituting and Erect-
> ing such other Courts of Record as her Maj-
> esty her heirs and Successors by her or
> their commissions or Instructions to her or
> their Governor or Commander in Chief of this
> Colony and Dominion for the time being shall
> direct.[27]

Three years later, Governor Spotswood reported that the

Assembly, acting upon his suggestion, had passed a clar-

ifying act stating that the Act of 1705 was never to be

interpreted as in any way infringing upon the judicial

prerogatives of the crown.[28]

---

27. Board of Trade to the Governor and Council of
Virginia, March 25, 1707, PRO CO5/1362, Va. Col. Rec.
microfilm.

28. Spotswood to the Lord of Trade, March 6, 1710,
PRO CO5/1363, Va. Col. Rec. microfilm; R. A. Brock, ed.,
The Official Letters of Alexander Spotswood, Lieutenant-

Courts of oyer and terminer, for which the Board of Trade had expressed concern, had not been unknown in seventeenth-century Virginia, for in 1662 Governor Berkeley's instructions had granted, in answer to his specific request, a commission of oyer and terminer. But this authorization had been accompanied with the suggestion that should the governor and Assembly think it necessary and requisite to establish such courts for the better execution of justice, and if the Assembly would appropriate a suitable salary, "some persons Learned in the Laws" would be sent from England to act as judges. But the colony had little intention of providing additional salaries for positions that would be filled by crown appointments, and those courts of oyer and terminer that were held were more in the nature of courts martial than trials, as witness the summary justice dealt Bacon's rebels. In 1671, Thomas Shaw, condemned to hang by a court of oyer and terminer, had been reprieved a full year (until the meeting of the next April General Court) to determine if the king would bestow his mercy. And the 1682 instructions to Lord

---

Governor of the Colony of Virginia, 1710-1722 (Richmond, 1932-1935), I, 49-50; Hening, Statutes, III, 489-490; JHB 1702-1712, pp. 266-267.

Culpeper authorized him to establish courts of judicature with the advice of Council, and more specifically, to issue commissions of oyer and terminer to county courts for the trial of slaves accused of a felony. Governor Nicholson, in 1699, was granted the power to issue commissions of oyer and terminer to try pirates, privateers and others accused of crimes on the high seas.[29]

One of the first references to a court of oyer and terminer in the eighteenth century occurred April 20, 1706, when the Council advised the governor to issue a commission of oyer and terminer for the trial of Anne Peacock, spinster of Richmond County, charged with the concealment of the death of her bastard child. This was the result of a postponement of the original trial in the General Court at the request of the attorney-general, who

---

29. "Instructions to Berkeley, 1662," Virginia Magazine of History and Biography, III (July, 1896), p. 20; McIlwaine, Minutes of the General Court, pp. 252, 259; Virginia Magazine of History and Biography, XXVI (July, 1918), 260-261; Hening, Statutes, III, 178. Governor Berkeley, in 1671, reported that the governor and his sixteen councillors held commissions of oyer and terminer. (Hening, Statutes, II, 511.) Such commissions, however, could well be similar to those mentioned in 1682, when it was stated that persons on trial for their life, and who could not be brought to trial on the fourth day of the General Court, could be tried any time during the sitting of the General Court or meeting of the Assembly under a commission of oyer and terminer. (Ibid., I, 35.)

had discovered his witnesses not yet ready to testify and their evidence "not of weight to find her guilty." Yet it was felt that holding the prisoner until the next sitting of the General Court would not only prove a hardship on the defendant, but would "be a great charge to the Country...."[30]

Such instances, however, seem to have been the exception rather than the rule, and it was not until 1710 that specific instructions to Governor Alexander Spotswood directed the regular appointments of courts of oyer and terminer as the most expeditious method of disposing of the cases of freemen accused of criminal actions. In Spotswood's proclamation, the Virginians were not only notified that they had been extended the rights of habeas corpus by Queen Anne, but Her Majesty had likewise charged him with the appointment of two annual courts of oyer and terminer, to be supported from the public treasury, which were to meet on the first Tuesdays of December and June. Innocent enough on the surface, there lay in this directive the basis

---

30. Exec. Jour. Council Col. Va., III, 82.

for the most violent jurisdictional dispute in the history of the colony.[31]

This matter was first referred by the Council to the General Court--literally to themselves. The court held that public notices should announce that the first such court of oyer and terminer would be held the first Tuesday in December, 1710, and they suggested to the General Assembly that witnesses, jurors and venires be granted the same exemptions as existed for the General Court.[32]

The House of Burgesses, in turn, asked that they be allowed to examine the pertinent paragraphs in Spotswood's instructions, and came to the conclusion that no specific action was required by that body. The consensus was that the Act of 1710, clarifying the General Court Act of 1705, which stated that the sovereign's right to establish courts of oyer and terminer within the colony was not to be impaired, was in itself an

---

31. York County Records, Orders, Wills, &c., XIV, 80-81, Virginia State Library, Richmond, Virginia; [Lyon G. Tyler],"Writ of Habeas Corpus," William and Mary Quarterly, 1st series, III (January, 1895), 151-153.

32. Exec. Jour. Council of Col. Va., III, 250, 255.

adequate instrument for the sanctioning of such courts.[33]

Spotswood, at best a petulant man, demonstrated his displeasure in December, 1712, by issuing a commission for a court of oyer and terminer and naming as judges six members of the Council and three non-members, the latter including the speaker and two other members of the House of Burgesses. The councillors, nursing bruised sensibilities, declared that since the beginning of the colony they had held jurisdiction over all trials in which the punishments involved the loss of life or limb. In their protest they charged that the governor had introduced "Foreign'rs into the Courts of Judicature in this Colony." In answer Spotswood replied that there were certainly no foreigners in the county courts, or in the General Court, while in courts of oyer and terminer, "the Councill have usually been the judges also."[34]

---

33. William P. Palmer and others, eds., Calendar of Virginia State Papers and Other Manuscripts, 1652-1781, (Richmond, 1875), I, 143-144; Spotswood to the Lords of Trade, March 20, 1718, PRO CO5/1318, Va. Col. Rec. microfilm.

34. Spotswood to the Lords of Trade, received May 11, 1717, PRO CO5/1318, Va. Col. Rec. microfilm; Spotswood to the Lords of Trade, February 7, 1716, Brock, Spotswood Letters, II, 192-193; Spotswood to the Lords of Trade, March 20, 1718, PRO CO5/1318, Va. Col. Rec. microfilm.

The quarrel continued over the next several years. The Council carried their unhappiness with the governor into the courtroom, so much so that Spotswood withdrew from the bench "on account of the rude & unrighteous behaviour of most of the present Remonstrants." The absence of the presiding officer so disrupted the normal proceedings that the grand jury, in October, 1716, submitted a formal request to the sulking governor that he return to the court because of "our Concern to See our fellow Subjects so long deprived of one of the most essential branches of your Administration by your absence from the Generall Court bench."[35]

This continuing argument revolved around interpretation of the law. Spotswood sent the Board of Trade an abstract of complaints, and when the dispute was decided in his favor the councillors were so incensed that the governor sent the Board a complete text, complaining that the Council persisted in their triple roles of legislators, councillors and judges while attempting to draw a delicate line of thinking between each. Then

---

35. Grand Jury to Alexander Spotswood, October, 1716, PRO CO5/1318, Va. Col. Rec. microfilm.

too, he went on, there had been cases where the defendant had claimed kin to so many of the judges that a
trial could not be pressed in the General Court for lack
of impartial judges.[36]

The spokesman for the Council was William
Byrd II, who had been intriguing for the governor's post
when Spotswood was appointed. Byrd, who referred to
Spotswood as "arroganti," presented the Council's arguments before the Board of Trade in 1717. The crux of
their statement was that ever since the beginning of the
colony the Governor and the Council, by common usage,
had held the sole right to try all cases whose punishments involved the loss of life or limb; therefore the
governor had no right to appoint judges who were not
members of the Council to a commission of oyer and
terminer. This power of appointment, Byrd argued,
placed dangerous authority in the hands of the executive in

> that Governors are not in the least exempt
> from humane frailty, Such as a passionate
> love for money, Resentment against such as

---

36. Spotswood to the Board of Trade, n.d. [received
May, 1717], PRO CO5/1318 and same to same, n.d. [received
August 23, 1717], PRO CO5/1314, Va. Col. Rec. microfilm.

presume to oppose their Designs, partiality to their Creatures and Favorites,
and many other Passions, to which men in
power are more Subject than other people.[37]

Nor was this all, for the governor held the right to

appoint judges without the advice of Council.

In rebuttal, Spotswood declared that the argu-

ments were made plausible only by "reaping up the old

defective Acts of Virginia," and they had managed to

twist their charter into strange and wondrous interpre-

tations. He based the popularity of his stand on the

fact that the grand jury had petitioned his return to

the bench of the General Court.[38]

The House of Burgesses, fearful of any enlarge-

ment of the power of the governor, entered the dispute

on the side of the Council, even though the appointment

of three of their members to the court had touched off

the quarrel. A paper based on the grievances cited

---

37. William Byrd to the Lords of Plantations, n.d.,
PRO CO5/1318, Va. Col. Rec. microfilm. This remonstrance
in Cal. Va. St. Papers, I, 190-193, is dated 1718, but
this is in error inasmuch as this letter was received in
London, October 10, 1717 and read before the Board, November 13, 1717.

38. Spotswood to the Lords of Trade, March 20,
1718, PRO CO5/1318, Va. Col. Rec. microfilm.

against the courts of oyer and terminer was drawn up by
the opponents of the governor, and circulated throughout
the colony for signatures. To attract additional support,
the grievances against the executive were coupled with a
popular cause, the statutory regulation of official fees.
When only two counties returned these petitions, signed
only with a total of twenty-nine names, "all very obscure
fellows," Spotswood interpreted this apathy of the people
as a reluctance to increase the political factions within
the Council. In the subsequent elections, however, the
Council "by great Industry, and practices usual in the
Elections, got many of their Relations, and some others
of weak Understandings and credulous Tempers chosen for
Burgesses, [and] upon the meeting of the Assembly, these
appeared a Majority of the Party...."[39]

The Burgesses almost immediately resolved that
an address to the king should be drawn up repeating a
number of the Council's grievances. They expressed apprehension that unless the governor's authority be curbed
he would be able to exercise dictatorial powers which,

---

39. Spotswood to the Lords of Trade, June 24, 1718,
Brock, Spotswood Letters, II, 276-277.

in turn, would lead to a state in which "the Governour
may have the lives and Estates of your Majesties good
Subjects of this Colony very much in his power and will
be able to defeat the Jurisdiction of your Majesties
Said Generall Court whenever he shall think fit." Main-
taining that only the king could defeat "the Designs of
your Enemys," they implored the monarch "to restrain
this Dangerous power."[40]

In the meantime, the Board of Trade, disturbed
by the intensity of the quarrel, had submitted the case
to the attorney-general of England. After delivering
his opinion upon the legality of Spotswood's stand,
that official noted "what remain are only Arguments ab
Inconvenienti and from the fatal Consequences represented
to be, if the Governor should have power to appoint
Judges to Try People for their Lives." As an antidote
for the Council's opposition he suggested that since
their complaints

> are not Arguments against the Power but
> against the Use of it, and Peradventure
> in Case of bad Governours there might be
> such Consequences at a Distance from
> England,...His Majesty may be pleased
> for the preventing of Inconveniencies,

---

40. JHB 1712-1726, pp. 194, 208.

and Quieting the Minds of His Subjects there,
by His Instructions to the Governour, to Restrain his power of Issuing Special Commissions
of Oyer and Terminer, Except in Cases of extraordinary Emergencies, and in the Vacancy of
the General Court.[41]

One of Spotswood's primary antagonists was removed from the local scene when William Byrd went to
London as agent for the colony, but Byrd still fought
the Council's battle, and even entered into some intrigue
to get himself appointed governor of Virginia. Upon
Byrd's departure Spotswood had strengthened his support
by nominating as a replacement on the Council, Cole
Digges, the governor declaring Digges' best qualification
to be "that he is in no way related to that Luck of Hundred that sway the Bench in the Generall Court,...[and]
are a very Great Grievance to all the People here who
are not of the same Party." Although the councillors,
on three separate occasions, had their arguments struck
down by the English government, they persisted in main-
taining the struggle against what they considered an
usurpation of their privileges. On the surface, it

41. Opinion of the Attorney-General to Lords of
Trade and Plantations, December 24, 1717, PRO CO5/1318,
Va. Col. Rec. microfilm.

appeared that they had accepted defeat, but Spotswood noted that they had "Spirited up a Party" in the House of Burgesses and still referred to the governor "as an Oppressor and Subverter of their Constitution...." The only solution, he concluded, that would allow Virginia to "enjoy in quiet the fruits of that Plenty and Peace, w'ch it now more remarkably possesses than since its being a Colony," was for the king to break up the faction in the Council by removing some of the more militant members.[42]

This controversy, lasting eight years, seems to have been finally settled in 1720. In May of that year Spotswood reported that all differences were

> now entirely accomodated to the General
> Satisfaction of the Country, the Chief
> point in Controversy being that of the Gov-
> ernor's power of nominating Judges of Oyer
> and Terminer, those Gent'n who had contended
> for the Right of the Council to be the sole
> Judges in those Courts have, since the last
> hearing of their pretensions before ye King
> in Council, thought fit to fall into more
> moderate Sentiments, and as I had often

---

42. Spotswood to Lords of Trade and Plantations, March 25, 1718, Brock, Spotswood Letters, II, 304; same to same, March 25, 1719, ibid., II, 313; same to same, May 26, 1719, ibid., II, 320-321; Louis B. Wright and Marion Tinling, eds., The London Diary, 1717-1721, and Other Writings of William Byrd of Virginia (New York, 1958), p. 238.

laboured to such a Temper, I embraced with
a great deal of Satisfaction the occasion
that was offered to drop all past contentions,
and to unite again for the publick service,
and even all private Resentments are Abolished
w'th the publick Contests, and no more
Invidious Distinctions left of Governor's
and Country's Partys, I doubt not to get
such an Assembly, wherein I shall be able
to obtain many things for the King's Service and the benefite of the Colony, w'ch I
have been hitherto obstructed in.[43]

Spotswood had legally won his fight to retain
the appointive power, yet the Council did not lose. By
1726 commissions for the courts of oyer and terminer were
naming only councillors as judges, while from 1727 on the
governor himself was not a member of these courts, his
only concerns were issuing the commissions and signing
the death warrants. By 1755 this procedure had so
crystalized that Governor Robert Dinwiddie reported that
judges of the courts of oyer and terminer were "only such
as are members of the Council." The most positive evidence of the complete victory of the Council over the
governor was recorded by Lord Adam Gordon when he visited
Virginia in 1765 and who, after noting the Council members to be also the judges of the courts of oyer and

_____

43. Spotswood to Secretary Craggs, May 20, 1720,
Brock, Spotswood Letters, II, 341.

terminer, observed, "there [their] powers are greater

than those of any other Province, and they have no

Chief Justice."[44]

Aside from this great controversy, there were

few deviations from the norm. In 1741 there was a dis-

pute when the jealously guarded prerogatives of the

Council seemed to be threatened. Robert Dinwiddie,

later to become governor of Virginia, was appointed

surveyor-general of the southern part of North America.

As such, his commission entitled him to seats in the

Councils of Virginia, North Carolina and South Carolina.

After he had been admitted as a member of the Council by

Governor William Gooch, the other members limited him to

an advisory capacity, refusing to allow him to act as

either a member of the upper house or a judge of the

---

44. Drysdale to the Lords of Trade, June 29, 1726, PRO CO5/1320, Va. Col. Rec. microfilm; William Gooch to his brother, December 29, 1727, Gooch typescripts, Colonial Williamsburg, Inc.; Dinwiddie to Lords of Trade, January, 1755, R. A. Brock, ed., The Official Papers of Robert Dinwiddie, Lieutenant-Governor of the Colony of Virginia, 1751-1758 (Richmond, 1933), I, p. 384; Lord Adam Gordon, "Journal of an Officer who Travelled in America and the West Indies in 1764 and 1765," Newton D. Mereness, ed., Travels in the American Colonies (New York, 1916), p. 403; Spotswood to the Board of Trade, October 22, 1720, Brock, Spotswood Letters, II, 343-344; William A. R. Goodwin, The Record of Bruton Parish Church, ed. by Mary Goodwin (Richmond, 1941), p. 92.

General Court. This objection held some logic inasmuch as the office of surveyor-general required Dinwiddie to travel and his attendance would be always in doubt; because of the broad demands of his position, his familiarity with Virginia laws would be slim, and because he owned no property in Virginia, his concern for the colony would be lessened, "as their regards for their country must flow from the enjoyment of their properties." These arguments of the Council made so much sense that the following year Dinwiddie was issued a commission as an "ordinary" councillor.[45]

As the colony expanded, so did litigation. The docket of the General Court was so loaded with cases awaiting adjudication that the judges could not hear them all in the eighteen days provided for in the General Court Act of 1705. In February, 1745, the General Assembly advanced the opening day of the court from the fifteenth to the tenth of April and October and increased

---

45. William Gooch to his brother, December 28, 1727, and June 28, 1729, Gooch typescripts, CWI; Dinwiddie to the Board of Trade, October 20, 1741, Virginia Council to the Board of Trade, November 6, 1741, Louis K. Koontz, ed., Robert Dinwiddie Correspondence Illustrative of his Career in American Colonial Government and Westward Expansion, published on microfilm by the University of California Press (Berkeley, 1951), pp. 17-18, 25-33.

the overall period of the session from eighteen to twenty-four days, excluding Sundays.[46]

Less than a year after this law went into effect in May, 1746, disaster struck. On the morning of January 30, 1747, the Capitol was destroyed by fire. Governor William Gooch, through a proclamation dated April 6, 1747, declared that the General Court would sit as usual, temporary quarters having been secured in the old theatre building which the City of Williamsburg had but recently acquired and remodelled into a hustings court.[47]

As in the case of the burning of the last statehouse at Jamestown, the destruction of the Capitol in Williamsburg led many to think of removing the capital to a more convenient location. Not only was the question of distance argued, but such things as the unsalutary nature of the climate and water at Williamsburg, and the high cost of living were brought up. And, it was declared, the morals of the students of William and Mary were being "greatly depraved by the evil Examples they

---

46. Hening, Statutes, V, 319-320

47. Exec. Jour. Council Col. Va., V, 490-491.

see from the Numbers that flock to this Place at the public Meetings, the Impressions that are receiv'd at those Times being too strong for all the Care of the Masters to overcome." The dispute raged for some time, but the governor and several prominent citizens of the community fought to keep the capital in Williamsburg, their most powerful argument being that the city was free from the smallpox that was ravaging the rest of the colony at this time. The "Royal Fabric," or new Capitol, utilizing the old walls, was completed in 1753.[48]

Even before their new quarters were completed the General Court found themselves involved in another dilemma. In 1748 an act passed the Assembly relative to the proceedings of the General Court, the bill having been prepared by the committee for the revisal of the laws. This was one of ten Virginia statutes disallowed by the crown and was made known through a proclamation by Governor Dinwiddie on April 8, 1752. This disallowance, in effect, declared all proceedings of the General Court between 1748 and 1752 null and void.

---

48. Hening, Statutes, VI, 197-198; Legis. Jour. Council Col. Va., II, 1037-1038.

Despite the dismay generated by the disallowance, the
Assembly took quick and forceful action. Adopting the
recommendations of a joint committee both houses passed,
the same day, a bill declaring valid the "process and
proceedings of the General Court between the commence-
ment and repealing of the act...." A similar joint
committee petitioned the king for a reconsideration of
his action, explaining that the disallowed act was little more than a compilation of former acts, and only
minor changes had been made "for the Ease of the Court,
the Benefit of the Suitors, and the Convenience of Attorneys...." Although aware that a law, once disallowed by
the crown, could not be repassed by a colonial legislature, acknowledging "a just Sense of your Majesty's Wis-
dom in repealing certain of our revised Laws," the Virginians suggested that in this instance a reconsideration
was imperative. In response to these pleas George II
instructed Dinwiddie that he was amenable to a repassage
of the two bills concerning the General Court. In February, 1752, the new General Court Act was passed with
only a few minor changes from the original.[49]

---

49. Hening, Statutes, VI, 229-230; JHB 1742-1769,
pp. xiv-xv; Legis. Jour. Council Col. Va., II, 1082-1083,
1085.

This was the last change of any consequence in the development of the General Court of colonial Virginia. There were, of course, disruptions during the Stamp Act and similar crises in the succeeding years, but by the middle of the eighteenth century the majority of the laws, customs, precedents and proceedings with respect to the General Court had fallen into a fairly static pattern. The original intent of the early authorities seems to have been that the courts should have been modelled on English judicial institutions. They were indeed, but the end product bore little resemblance to the model, for the exigencies of a colonial civilization brought about certain mutations to fit a raw environment.

Chapter II

THE GENERAL COURT: ITS JURISDICTION AND PERSONNEL

The General Court of colonial Virginia func-

tioned as the supreme judicial unit of the colony and

was possessed of unusually extensive jurisdictional

authority.   Its broad legal scope was outlined in the

General Court Act of November, 1753:

> That the said general court shall take
> cognizance of, and are hereby declared to
> have power and jurisdiction to hear and de-
> termine, all causes, matters, and things
> whatsoever, relating to, or concerning any
> person or persons, ecclesiastical or civil,
> or to any person or things, of what nature
> soever the same shall be, whether brought
> before them by original process, appeal from
> any inferior court, or by any other ways or
> means whatsoever.[1]

---

1.   William Waller Hening, ed., The Statutes at Large:
Being a Collection of all the Laws of Virginia from the
First Session of the Legislature, in the Year 1619 (New
York, 1810-1823), VI, 327.   Although the General Court tried
few ecclesiastical cases, such procedure was not unknown.
Governor Dinwiddie and his Council, sitting as a court
in 1757, tried the Reverend John Brumskill, the minister
for Hamilton Parish in Prince William County.   Brumskill
was convicted of "monstrous Immorality, profane Swearing,
drunkenness & very immoral actions," and forbidden to act

The primary appellate function of the General
Court lay in hearing appeals from the county courts.
Inasmuch as this was a relatively easy and inexpensive
process, the docket of the higher court was often clut-
tered with appeals from the decisions of the county justices. And it was because of these "frivolous suits in
the general court, and trifling and vexatious appeals
from the county courts and other inferiour courts"
that legislation in 1761 prohibited lawyers practicing
in both the county courts and the General Court.[2]

---

as minister for any parish in Virginia. (Robert Dinwiddie
to the Bishop of London, September 12, 1757, Fulham Palace
Papers 15, Virginia Colonial Records Project microfilm,
Colonial Williamsburg, Inc.)

2. Hening, Statutes, VII, 399. A similar statute
had been passed as early as 1748. Under this earlier
law, attorneys with General Court licenses were still
allowed to practice in the courts of York, James City,
Warwick, Elizabeth City and Gloucester Counties, and the
Hustings Court of Williamsburg, presumably because of
the proximity of these courts to the General Court in
Williamsburg. In 1757 this restriction was eliminated,
and for the next four years, lawyers were allowed to
practice in both the superior and inferior courts of the
colony. (Ibid., VI, 143, VII, 124-125.) Thomas Jefferson,
in 1779, furnished a key to this prohibition when he wrote,
"I think the bar of the general court a proper and an ex-
cellent nursery for future judges....But this can never
be if an inundation of insects is permitted to come from
the county courts and consume the harvest. These people
traversing the counties seeing the clients frequently at
their own courts or perhaps at their own houses must of

In original jurisdiction, the General Court was enjoined from hearing civil cases involving less than £10 or 2,000 pounds of tobacco. Specific penalties were listed to prevent the use of the high court for the settlement of trivial litigation. There was, however, an exception to this rule. Suits of smaller valuation could be initiated in the General Court against vestrymen and county justices of the peace.[3] Since vestrymen and county justices were responsible for the administration of both ecclesiastical and temporal law in the counties, it was reckoned that it would be difficult to obtain an impartial decision in the inferior courts dominated by these men.

In criminal cases the General Court held jurisdiction over all arraignments involving the loss of life or limb as a punishment.[4] Because of the severity of

---

necessity pick up all the business. The convenience of frequently seeing their counsel without going from home cannot be withstood by the country people." (Julian Boyd, ed., The Papers of Thomas Jefferson [Princeton, 1950-], II, 235.)

3. Hening, Statutes, V, 327-328.

4. By a law of 1655/56, persons charged with a crime carrying this penalty could be tried by either the General Court or the General Assembly, whichever met first. (Ibid., I, 398.) The records do not reveal that the Assembly ever exercised this privilege.

colonial laws, all felonies, therefore, were decided before the superior court. The only exceptions were the
case of slaves accused of capital crimes; slaves so
charged were tried before a court of oyer and terminer
by the county justices by virtue of a special commission
issued by the governor.[5]

The General Court sat twice a year, on April
10th and October 10th, provided those dates did not fall
on a Sunday; in such an event the session began the following Monday. Each session was to continue for twenty-four
days (Sundays excepted) or until the docket had been
cleared. After 1753, the first five days of every court
session were devoted to the hearing and determining cases
in chancery and appeals from the inferior courts. The
remaining nineteen days were to be taken up in "trying
suits or prosecutions on behalf of his majesty, and all
other matters whatsoever, there depending...."[6]

---

5. Hening, Statutes, III, 102-103.

6. Ibid., V, 319-320. Prior to 1745 the General
Court met on April 15th and October 15th for eighteen
days, excluding Sundays. (Ibid., III, 289, V, 319-320.)
The eighth day of the session was sometimes referred to
as "Criminal Day." (Virginia Gazette, October 10, 1745.)
The fourth day was designated as the day for criminal
trials in 1662. (Hening, Statutes, II, 63.) However,

There is some difficulty in determining just
what hours the judges of the General Court sat on the
bench. A law of 1662 stated that the hours of the
court were to be between eight and eleven in the fore-
noon and from one to three in the afternoon. Yet it appears that these restrictions were flexible and there was
little adherence to the strict letter of the law. Among
the several charges brought against Governor Nicholson
in 1703 was that he kept the court sitting until "unreasonable hours of the night."   In later years, during
William Byrd II's tenure, attendance seems to have been
equally erratic. Between 1711 and 1741 Byrd records
varying hours as the time of his arrival at court. Of
these, ten and eleven in the morning were the most popular, but it appears that the court had often gone into
session before his appearance. The hours of adjournment
likewise were not consistent, although four o'clock in
the afternoon seems to have been the most popular. Yet,

---

in 1718, Governor Spotswood complained that the councillors
"do not try Criminals on the fourth day of the Court as
that Law [General Court Law of 1705] positively enjoines,
but only Arraign them according to the Tenour of the Revised Law." (Spotswood to the Lords of Trade, March 20,
1718, PRO CO5/1318, Va. Col. Rec. microfilm.) In 1753
the sixth day was designated as "Criminal Day." (Hening,
Statutes, VI, 329.)

upon one occasion Byrd noted in his diary, "We sat till it grew dark and dispatched a great deal of business." But this was an exception, and more often the court rose in the early afternoon.[7]

The judges of this superior court were the most powerful men in the colony, for the bench of the General Court was composed of the members of the Governor's Council with the governor as the presiding officer. Any five formed a quorum. The prerogative of the Council to act as judges of the highest court in Virginia dated back to the Charter of 1618. Council members received their commissions from the king, issued over his "sign manual." Normally, their appointment was the result of a recommendation by the governor, but it was not unknown that a candidate receive his position on the Council through the connivance of an influential friend in England. Council members held their offices during good behavior, which,

---

7. Hening, Statutes, II, 61; Philip Ludwell to James Blair, October 21, 1703, PRO CO5/1314, Va. Col. Rec. microfilm; "Answer of James Thrall in Behalf of Nicholson," Virginia Magazine of History and Biography, VII (April, 1900), 387; Louis B. Wright and Marion Tinling, eds., The Secret Diary of William Byrd of Westover, 1709-1712 (Richmond, 1941), pp. 332, 427, 428, 519, 520-521; Maude H. Woodfin and Marion Tinling, eds., Another Secret Diary of William Byrd of Westover, 1730-1741, With Letters & Literary Exercises, 1696-1726 (Richmond, 1942), pp. 58, 165.

for all practical purposes, usually meant that they held
the position for life. During the seventeenth century
the membership of the Council had fluctuated from two to
eighteen, but in the eighteenth century the body was
limited to twelve men.[8]

Seldom were these twelve men skilled in the law.
In 1717, William Byrd went so far as to admit their ignorance in the statement, "Indeed I rest upon the absurdity
of men judging over matters of Law which they do not understand, which every body Knows is the case with most of us
Councillors...." Primarily, they were "the principal
Gentlemen of the Colony," or perhaps more accurately,
"the most opulent and landed men of the province...."

---

8. Hening, Statutes, III, 288, VI, 326; Francis
Fauquier, "Answer to the Queries sent by the Lords of
Trade and Plantations" [c. 1764], Huntington Library, San
Marino, California; York County Records, Orders, Wills,
&c., XIV, 80-81, Virginia State Library, Richmond, Virginia; Dinwiddie to the Lords of Trade, January, 1755, R. A.
Brock, ed., The Official Papers of Robert Dinwiddie, Lieutenant-Governor of the Colony of Virginia, 1751-1758 (Richmond, 1933), I, 98-110, 383; William Stith, The History of
the First Discovery and Settlement of Virginia: Being an
Essay Towards a General History of this Colony (Williamsburg, 1747), appendix, pp. 23-24; Gooch to the Lord of
Trade, February 12, 1730/31, PRO CO5/1322, Va. Col. Rec.
microfilm; R. A. Brock, ed., The Official Letters of
Alexander Spotswood, Lieutenant-Governor of the Colony
of Virginia, 1710-1722 (Richmond, 1932-1935), II, 39-40;
Virginia Magazine of History and Biography, XXI (October,
1913), 389; William and Mary Quarterly, 1st series, III

The reasoning behind the selection of the landed gentry
as judges is perhaps best explained in an observation
made by Governor Gooch in 1730. He noted that as men
of property they were "thought by everybody the only fit
persons to judge the property of others."[9] By reason of
the frequent intermarriages between the families of the
members of the Council, there were recurring charges of
favoritism in the courts. As early as 1718, Governor
Alexander Spotswood was complaining bitterly of the
partiality shown by "that Luck of Hundred that sway the
Bench in the General Court." Just the year before, so
many judges were related to Colonel Ludwell, who had a
case before the court, that out of the ten then present,

(July, 1894), 15, 232; Percy Scott Flippin, The Royal
Government in Virginia, 1624-1775 (New York, 1919),
p. 156. From an examination of the executive journals
of the Council, it appears that they assumed extra-legal
powers and sometimes acted as an informal court while
sitting as a Council. They settled a number of disputes
in this manner.

9. Fauquier, "Answers to the Queries" [1764],
Huntington Library; Josiah Quincy, Memoir of the Life
of Josiah Quincy Jun: of Massachusetts (Boston, 1825),
p. 128; Byrd to Ludwell, September 24, 1717, Lee-Ludwell
Papers, Virginia Historical Society, Richmond, Virginia;
Gooch to the Lords of Trade, March 26, 1730, PRO CO5/1321,
Va. Col. Rec. microfilm.

a quorum could not be assembled to try the case. And
nine years later Governor Drysdale was warning the Lords
of Trade against putting "the power of Judicature in the
Genll Court too much into one Family." In justice to
the members of the court, however, it should be pointed
out that a judge was supposed to disqualify himself, and
usually did, when a case involving personal interests or
those of a relative appeared on the docket. Manifesta-
tions of partiality seem to have virtually disappeared
by 1773 when a critical Josiah Quincy observed that the
judge's "views, connexions, interests, or inclinations,
have generally been such, as to keep them from baser
betrayments of their trust, and the more atrocious pros-
titution of their enormous power and authority."[10]

The members of the Council, after 1753, received a total of £1200 annually, apportioned according
to their attendance at the Council and General Court.
Similarly, £100 was divided among the judges and other
officers of each court of oyer and terminer. An absent

---

10. Spotswood to the Lords of Trade, September 27,
1718, Brock, Spotswood Letters, II, 304; Spotswood to the Board
of Trade, August 23, 1717, PRO CO5/1364; and Drysdale to
the Lords of Trade, June 29, 1726, PRO CO5/1320, Va. Col.
Rec. microfilm; Quincy, Memoir, p. 128.

Council member was required to make his excuses by letter.
As a quorum of only five judges was necessary to conduct
a court, it seems that the members of the Council often
rotated active duty on the bench; thus each man could receive his share of the annual Council budget and still enjoy some freedom from attendance at the General Court.
There was one instance when the quorum suffered an unex-
pected reduction. Dr. William Cocke, Secretary of the
Colony and a member of the Council, was seized with an
"Applectick fitt," while serving as a judge and died
immediately.[11]

The governor, when actively sitting on the bench,
served as chief justice. It was his responsibility to
preside over the court, charge the jury, and pass sentence upon the convicted. But there his authority ended.

---

11. Dinwiddie to Sir Thomas Robinson, October 25,
1754, Brock, Dinwiddie Papers, I, 253; Dinwiddie's Report to
the Lords of Trade, January, 1755, ibid., I, 390; H. R.
McIlwaine and Wilmer L. Hall, ed., Executive Journals of
the Council of Colonial Virginia (Richmond, 1925-1945),
III, 280, V, 441, 469; Byrd, Secret Diary, pp. 336, 428;
Spotswood to the Lords of Trade, October 20, 1720, Brock,
Spotswood Letters, II, 343-344; William A. R. Goodwin,
The Record of Bruton Parish Church, ed. by Mary Goodwin
(Richmond, 1941), p. 92. Prior to 1753 the salary for
the Council had been £600. Apparently the pay for the
Council members was based on attendance at the General
Court rather than Council meetings. In 1708 William

Just as any councillor, he had only one vote, and there was no veto power, for the verdict rested on a majority vote of the judges. In the governor's absence, the president of the Council became the presiding officer of the court. As for courts of oyer and terminer, the governor was "no further concerned than granting a Com.[mission] to the Council & signing dead warrants." These courts were usually presided over by the president of the Council; in his absence, the first person named in the commission of oyer and terminer officiated in that capacity.[12]

The chief legal officer of the General Court was the attorney-general. During the seventeenth century this office was filled by an appointment from the king, but from around 1700 until near the end of the colonial era, he was appointed and commissioned by the

---

Byrd recommended that they be paid "in proportion to their whole attendance at the Council and General Courts," inasmuch as the councillors were always present for the court, but were not so "zealous" in their attendance at Council meetings (William Byrd to Blathwayt, September 21, 1708, Blathwayt Papers, Colonial Williamsburg, Inc.

12. William Gooch to Thomas Gooch, February 18, 1727, Gooch typescripts, Colonial Williamsburg, Inc.; Lewis Burwell to "My Lord," August 17, 1751, PRO CO5/1338, Va. Col. Rec. microfilm.

governor under the seal of the colony. For a short period just prior to the Revolution, the appointment of this office once again reverted to the home government. After 1703 the attorney-general was required to take up residence in Williamsburg, and if he found it necessary to be absent from the capital, he was required to appoint a competent deputy to serve in the interim. Not only was he a functionary of the courts, but he usually attended the meetings of the Council, although he was not officially a member of that body. The power of the governor was more restricted in his control over the attorney-general than any other appointive official of the colony.[13]

The duties of the attorney-general were numerous and complex, making it necessary that he be a person of better than average legal ability and training. This was especially true since most of the judges were

---

13. Exec. Jour. Council Col. Va., II, 29-30; Spotswood to the Lords of Trade, March 9, 1714, Brock, Spotswood Letters, II, 61; Flippin, Royal Government in Virginia, pp. 321-322; Oliver Perry Chitwood, Justice in Colonial Virginia (Baltimore, 1905), p. 120. Governor Francis Nicholson apparently held little respect for the attorney-general of the Colony. (See p. 20 above.) On the other hand, the attorney-general did not always demonstrate the proper respect for the authority of the governor. Governor Gooch complained bitterly of that official's "vile treatment of me." (Gooch to his brother, March 8, 1735, Gooch typescripts, Colonial Williamsburg, Inc.)

unlettered in the law, and "very incompetent in a number of intricate points which must necessarily come before them to decide upon [and they] may make mistakes from whence result consequences that are very prejudicial to the interest of the people."[14] It was because of this professional inadequacy on the part of the judges that the attorney-general was frequently, by order of the Council, required to give an opinion and ruling on the letter of the law. On more intricate questions, other lawyers were oft-times called in to assist in matters of interpretation. Questionable decisions of the county courts were examined and searched for possible error by the attorney-general. Among his primary legal responsibilities were the drawing of indictments and the prosecution of criminals in the General Court and courts of oyer and terminer. In a like manner, it was his duty to present the government's case against those who refused to pay quit-rents, violated the laws of trade, or in any other manner disobeyed the statutes of the colony. In

---

14. Earl of Dunmore to Lord Dartmouth, March 18, 1774, Strachey Papers, Clements Library, Ann Arbor, Michigan. Dunmore wanted judges skilled in the law appointed and felt that "Justice could be carried to the Doors of the People."

addition, there were certain informal obligations outside the courtroom. Committee members of the House of
Burgesses were counselled in the periodic revisions of
the laws, while the Governor and Council were advised in
the preparation of proclamations, commissions and other
legal documents.[15]

The clerk of the General Court was responsible
for keeping records of the court, taking the depositions
of witnesses, the publication of court orders, issuance
of subpoenas, and the preparation of the docket. He
performed the same services for the courts of oyer and
terminer. Normally, the secretary of the colony would
act as clerk of the General Court, but this was impossible for that dignitary was usually a councillor and
therefore a judge. Thus these duties were performed by

15. George Webb, The Office and Authority of a
Justice of Peace....(Williamsburg, 1736), p. 113;
Virginia Gazette, October 24, 1751; Journals of the
House of Burgesses in Virginia 1695-1702 (Richmond,
1906-1915), p. 146 [hereafter cited as JHB plus date];
Exec. Jour. Council Col. Va., IV, 281-282; Virginia
Magazine of History and Biography, XXII (January, 1914),
29-30; William P. Palmer and others, eds., Calendar of
Virginia State Papers and Other Manuscripts, 1652-1781,
(Richmond, 1875), I, 73-74, 94, 100, 161; Flippen,
Royal Government in Virginia, pp. 322-323.

his clerk who was appointed by the secretary and paid
out of the revenues accruing to his office.[16]

The secretary of the colony was one of the most
powerful figures in the colonial government of Virginia.
His office was gained through an appointment from the
crown, although the governor retained the privilege of
recommending a candidate. With one exception, the
secretary was always a member of the Council. This
appointment was William Adair, who held the position
in absentia from 1743 to 1776. Adair had apparently purchased the position in expectation of reaping the finan-
cial rewards of the office while continuing his residence
in England. During his appointment his duties were performed by his deputy, Thomas Nelson of Yorktown, and even
then Nelson was always known as "Secretary" Nelson and
there is little reference in the records of the colony

---

16. Henry Hartwell, James Blair and Edward Chilton,
The Present State of Virginia and the College, ed. by
Hunter Farish (Williamsburg, 1940), p. 49; Drysdale to
the Lords of Trade, June 29, 1726, PRO CO5/1320, Va. Col.
Rec. microfilm; Virginia Gazette, October 24 and 31,
1751; Virginia Magazine of History and Biography, IX
(April, 1902), 375-382; Exec. Jour. Council Col. Va.,
V, 247.

to Adair. Nelson was elected to the House of Burgesses in 1746 and was himself elevated to the Council in 1749.[17]

The office of secretary entailed multiple duties, one writer commenting, "there is such a Medley in it, that its scarce credible...." He was, in the first place, custodian of all the records of Virginia: the proceedings of the General Court and other courts, legal papers, commissions (both civil and military), land warrants, wills and probates, writs of election, judicial writs, birth,marriage and death notices, licenses, and papers pertaining to fines, forfeitures, and

---

17. Fauquier, "Answers to the Queries" [1764], Huntington Library; Exec. Jour. Council Col. Va., V, 283; JHB 1742-1747, 1748-1749, pp. viii, ix; William and Mary Quarterly, 1st series, XX (July, 1911), 18; Hartwell, Blair and Chilton, Present State of Virginia, p. 51. The practice of purchasing government positions was not unknown as Robert Carter had paid £1500 to have his son, Adair's predecessor, named to the post in 1722. Before Adair received the appointment, William Beverley was writing a London merchant, Charles Smyth, requesting that he bid over £2,000 for Beverley's appointment as secretary. (William Beverley to Charles Smyth, August 9, 1742, William Beverley Letterbook, New York Public Library.) Thomas Nelson, a lawyer by profession, was nominated by Governor Gooch to be attorney-general shortly after he had accepted the position as Adair's deputy secretary. (William Gooch to the Secretary of State, June 27, 1743, PRO CO5/1337, Va. Col. Rec. microfilm.

maritime matters. He was custodian of the Great Seal of
the colony. Commissions of oyer and terminer, although
signed by the governor, were actually drawn and issued
by the secretary's office. The secretary also appointed
county clerks, claiming the privilege of "USAGE" rather
than statute, which patronage added much to his political
power. In 1726 it was estimated that one-half the members of the House of Burgesses were obligated to the
secretary because of the appointments he had made. The
monetary rewards of the office were equally attractive.
In 1764 Governor Fauquier estimated that the income of
the secretary's office (arising from all legal fees)
amounted to over £1,000 per year.[18]

The sheriff was the chief administrative officer of a court. Each county sheriff was appointed annually by the Governor and Council and was selected from
a list of three submitted by the justices of the county
concerned. To be recommended for the office the candidate
had to be a member of the county court, although he was

18. JHB 1702-1712, p. 345; Hartwell, Blair and
Chilton, Present State of Virginia, pp. 48-51; Drysdale
to the Lords of Trade, June 29, 1726, PRO CO5/1320, Va.
Col. Rec. microfilm; Fauquier, "Answers to the Queries"
[1764], Huntington Library.

no longer allowed to serve in a judicial capacity after his appointment. The sheriff was appointed for a term of one year, although this could be extended for one additional year at the pleasure of the governor. There was no sheriff, per se, for the General Court though it was necessary that such an officer be in attendance to empanel juries, serve writs and execute the orders of the court. In the seventeenth century, while the court sat at Jamestown, the officer in attendance was the sheriff of James City County.[19] After the removal of the capital to Williamsburg, the sheriff of York County assumed the duties of court officer as the capitol was located in the York County section of Williamsburg. There is no evidence of any law or directive calling for this change; it appears to have come about as a result of custom and precedent.

Not only the sheriff but the under-sheriffs of York County attended the General Court sessions. One of the duties of the sheriff was to empanel both the

---

19. Hening, Statutes, II, 78. The sheriff of each county was required to post a bond of £1500 before he assumed office. (Richard Starke, The Office and Authority of a Justice of Peace, Explained and Digested, Under Proper Titles [Williamsburg, 1774], p. 323.)

grand and petit juries, a task sometimes entrusted to

the under-sheriffs. For the under-sheriff this held some

of the elements of an occupational hazard, since in the

event he summoned a person ineligible for jury duty, he

was subject to a fine for his carelessness. Apparently

the sheriff of James City County often assisted in the

empaneling of a jury. The York County sheriff, however,

was granted some extra-territorial rights with respect

to the courts. Because of the division of Williamsburg

by the James City-York County line, he was allowed to

summon grand and petit jurors, take evidence, and execute

the commands of the court, not only within the limits of

Williamsburg, but for a half-mile radius around the town.

Among the other services performed by the attending

sheriff was the collection of all fines imposed by the

court, to be turned over to the receiver-general of the

colony. The regular income of the sheriff was derived

from ten per cent of all quit-rents collected, a percent-

age of all fees collected, and fees for certain duties

performed for the county courts, the amount of which was

specified by the Assembly. For his duties in attendance

at the General Court the York County sheriff was paid an allowance above his regular income.[20]

In addition to these major figures, there were certain minor officials necessary to insure the smooth operation of the General Court. Among these was the court cryer. Up until 1732 the functions of the cryer were performed by one of the under-sheriffs of York County. Because of the regular turnover in under-sheriffs (usually in office no longer than two years), it was necessary that they be trained in the duties of cryer at frequent intervals. It was with this in mind that the position of court cryer was created, with a salary of ten pounds sterling for each court. His appointment came from the governor.[21]

---

20. Exec. Jour. Council Col. Va., IV, 257, 284; Drysdale to the Lords of Trade, June 29, 1726, PRO CO5/ 1320, Va. Col. Rec. microfilm; Hening, Statutes, II, 146, V, 515-517; Dinwiddie to Lord Fairfax, May 6, 1752, Brock, Dinwiddie Papers, I, 21; Beverley, Present State of Virginia, pp. 199, 257; JHB 1702-1712, pp. 52, 137; JHB 1752-1758, p. 110; Fauquier, "Answers to the Queries" [1764], Huntington Library; Hartwell, Blair and Chilton, Present State of Virginia, pp. 27, 56; Webb, Justice of Peace, pp. 143, 305.

21. Journal of the Council, May 7, 1771, PRO CO5/ 1349, Va. Col. Rec. microfilm; Fauquier, "Answers to the Queries" [1764], Huntington Library.

The tipstaff was another of these minor court functionaries. His duties were comparable to those of the bailiff of modern courts, including acting as usher, messenger, and doorkeeper for the General Court. His appointment, as that of the cryer, came from the governor. In 1771, Tipstaff Christopher Ayscough seems to have felt there were encouraging connotations in his title, for the Council fired him for excessive drunkenness.[22]

The chaplain was a peripheral member of the court. As early as 1660 the House of Burgesses appointed a chaplain to read prayers before each day's session, and the minister appointed by the House also served the General Court. There seems to have been no routine established for the chaplain, and from the rather scanty records available, it would seem that his primary duty was preaching to the Council on those mornings they assumed the roles of judges. The chaplain also visited condemned prisoners in the public gaol, and it may be assumed that

---

22. Hening, Statutes, I, 549; JHB 1761-1765, pp. 34, 49, 67, 173, 205, 229; H. R. McIlwaine, ed., Legislative Journals of the Council of Colonial Virginia (Richmond, 1918-1919), III, 1391, 1396.

he offered them spiritual comfort on their last walk--to
the gallows.[23]

Another minor, yet necessary, official on the
fringe of the General Court was the gaoler. His appointment stemmed from the governor, albeit the consent of the
Council was always obtained before it was made. With his
appointment came the requirement that he post a £500 bond
"for the due execution of his office." The gaoler's
salary was not based on statute, but was based upon "such
allowance as by the general Assembly shall be thought
reasonable." His annual pay, granted each year by the
Assembly, ranged from fifteen pounds sterling in the
early part of the eighteenth century to around forty
pounds near the end of the colonial period. In addition,
there were certain fees and allowances that had been established by law payable to the gaoler. There were likewise certain prerogatives vested in the position. The

23. Virginia Gazette (Rind), November 23, 1769;
Cal. Va. St. Papers, I, 198; Byrd, Secret Diary, pp. 165,
452. It was ordered in 1721 that the "Ministers attending the Genl Court & Assemblys 40s Currt money for each
Sermon." (Exec. Jour. Council Col. Va., III, 540.) Later,
in 1737, because of the increased number of criminals this
was raised to an annual sum of £25 "Current money." (Ibid.,
IV, 398-399.) William Byrd's Diary suggests that he
usually attended church before he took his seat in the
court to assume his judicial duties.

gaoler was exempt from both militia and jury duty. On the other hand, there were certain liabilities. If the public gaoler permitted a prisoner to escape through an open door, or without the use of force on the part of the prisoner, or if allowed one of his charges to commit suicide, he could be charged with a felony.[24]

The duties of the gaoler were many. His principal charge was, of course, the imprisonment and care of persons charged with a violation of the laws or those already condemned and awaiting execution. During the actual sitting of the court his responsibilities were rather broadly defined by the law which stated he should "constantly attend and execute the commands of the general court...." Among other things, it was his duty to burn in the hand "in open court" all those who plead and were granted benefit of clergy. The gaoler was required to live close to his job, in quarters in the public gaol. And under the same roof he was responsible for the gaoling

---

24. Hening, Statutes, IV, 326, VI, 135-136; Exec. Jour. Council Col. Va., III, 222; JHB 1702-1712, p. 182; JHB 1761-1765, p. 20; Webb, Justice of Peace, pp. 169-170.

of debtors and runaway slaves as well as felons.[25]

These, then, were the men responsible for the
administration of justice in the highest court in colonial
Virginia. Not always trained and often lacking experience,
they exhibited such tenacity for a tough job that they
generally arrived at a successful conclusion despite their
deficiencies. As early as 1736 an anonymous observer was
noting that the courts of justice were conducted "with a
Dignity and Decorum, that would become them even in
Europe."[26] Indeed, it seems that the English propensity
to "muddle through" was one of the traits retained by
the colonists in the new world.

---

25. Hening, Statutes, IV, 326, VI, 106. After three
months in the public gaol, an unclaimed slave could be
hired out. First, however, an identifying iron collar
with the letters PG (Prisoner of the Gaol) stamped thereon,
was to be placed around his neck. (Ibid., VI, 365.) As a
point of interest, the placing of irons on prisoners and
striking them off seems to have been left to some crafts-
man of the community. In 1705, Thomas Whitby was perform-
ing this duty for the gaoler. (JHB 1702-1712, pp. 94-95.)

26. Anonymous, "Observations in Several Voyages and
Travels in America in the Year 1736," William and Mary
Quarterly, 1st series, XV (April, 1907), 223.

Chapter III

CRIMINAL TRIAL PROCEEDINGS IN THE GENERAL COURT

As in every civilization, colonial Virginia counted persons of criminal intent among its population. And an indicted felon, no matter where the locale of his alleged crime, was always brought to Williamsburg, there to be tried before the Council sitting as the General Court, the highest court in colonial Virginia. Originally, the proceedings of this court were based on English judicial customs, but throughout the years legal practices underwent a number of alterations to meet the exigencies of the local environment. So gradual were these changes that they were scarcely noted at the time, and people grew so accustomed to the proceedings of the court they could see no reasons for preserving on paper the manner in which these courts were conducted. And so it is, that to establish a pattern for justice in colonial criminal procedure, many small items from divers sources must be fitted together to form the final mosaic.

Once a felony was committed, it was the imme-
diate duty of every person who either witnessed or discovered the crime to inform the nearest justice of the
peace or constable. Should this crime involve death,
the coroner was likewise notified. Before the deceased
could be removed, it was necessary that a jury be assembled to "view the Body" and determine the cause of death.
It was the coroner's responsibility to issue a warrant
to the constable, empowering that peace officer to summon twenty-four freeholders to the spot where the body
lay. From this number, twelve jurors were chosen, one
of whom was appointed foreman by the coroner.[1]

The jurors sworn, the coroner delivered his
charge to the jury in which he outlined their

---

1. Richard Starke, The Office and Authority of a
Justice of Peace, Explained and Digested, Under Proper
Titles (Williamsburg, 1774), pp. 206-207; George Webb,
The Office and Authority of a Justice of Peace....(Wil-
liamsburg, 1736), pp. 97-104; H. R. McIlwaine, ed.,
Legislative Journals of the Council of Colonial Virginia
(Richmond,1918-1919), III, 1577. If the person informed
upon was convicted of a breach of penal law and the pen-
alty involved a forfeiture of goods, the informer re-
ceived one-half. (Starke, Justice of Peace, p. 220;
Webb, Justice of Peace, pp. 189-190; William Waller
Hening, ed., The Statutes at Large: Being a Collection
of all the Laws of Virginia from the First Session of
the Legislature, in the Year 1619 (New York, 1810-1823),
II, 189.)

responsibilities. The determination of the manner by
which the deceased met his or her death was their primary
function, but there were other considerations. If the
victim had been feloniously murdered, the jury was to
attempt to name his killer; determine just where the
killer was at the moment; and if the murderer was at
large, just what steps had been taken for his apprehension. If the jury decided that the deceased had taken
his own life, it was their duty to judge whether he had
been sane at the time of his death, as well as to determine the value of his "Goods and Chattels." This last
step was, in effect, a criminal proceeding, because suicide, or "Self-Murder," was considered a crime against
the crown. If the coroner's jury decided that the deceased was Felo de se, or "Felon of himself," they were
required to provide answers for four basic questions:
that he was "of the Age of Discretion"; that he was
Compos mentis, or of sound mind; that the act was voluntary; and that the death had occurred less than a year
and a day after the wound had been self-inflicted. If
all were decided in the affirmative, the goods and
chattels, but not the land, would be forfeited to the

crown. He was not, moreover, allowed a Christian burial.

A suicide adjudged _non compos mentis_, or insane, was not

subject to the penalties of the law.[2]

There was always the possibility that the victim had met his death by accident, and this, in turn, brought up the question of a deodand. A deodand was defined as a moveable object, animate or inanimate (a cart, boat, horse) instrumental in the death of a person. Objects fixed to a freehold, as a waterwheel or bell, were not considered deodands unless they became detached. In a like manner, a weapon used to kill in a murder was considered a deodand. In all cases, the deodand was subject to confiscation and usually sold, the proceeds turned over to the receiver-general, to be placed in the "casual revenue" of the colony. Customarily, by English practice, the proceeds realized from the sale of deodands were applied to the relief of the poor.[3]

---

2. Starke, _Justice of Peace_, p. 201; Webb, _Justice of Peace_, p. 237. If a person inflicted a wound upon himself and did not die of that wound within a year and a day, he could not be declared a suicide. The lands of a suicide were not forfeit, because land could be taken away only through an attainder (loss of civil rights and capacities, sentence of death, or outlawry), and by due process of law.

3. Starke, _Justice of Peace_, p. 128; Webb, _Justice of Peace_, p. 128. As an exception to this general rule,

Even more detail was required if the evidence suggested murder. The coroner's jury was required to literally view the body, a requisite that sometimes bordered on the unpleasant. Even if it had been found necessary to bury the deceased before the summoning of the jury, the body had to be exhumed to allow the jurors the opportunity of looking upon it. Once this gruesome task had been fulfilled, the jurors were allowed to retire to some more convenient spot for their deliberations. There witnesses could be sworn and examined, their testimony taken in writing and authenticated by their signatures or marks. If this testimony was considered vital to the subsequent examination of the accused by the county

---

the proprietors of the Northern Neck always claimed deodands in that area. (William Gooch to the Lords of Trade, n.d., Virginia Magazine of History and Biography, III [October, 1895], 116; Hening, Statutes, IV, 520.) When the confiscation of a deodand constituted a hardship upon the survivors of the deceased, the Council would sometimes recommend a return of the deodand. (H. R. McIlwaine and Wilmer L. Hall, eds., Executive Journals of the Council of Colonial Virginia (Richmond, 1925-1945, III, 153.) The custom of confiscating deodands was a relic of medieval custom. In those days it was considered a tragedy when a person came to a sudden and untimely end without an opportunity to confess his sins and receive absolution from the priest. The instrument of death, therefore, was turned over to the church, the proceeds of its sale turned over as alms to poor churchmen to pray the soul of the deceased out of Purgatory.

justices, the witness was bound by a "Recognizance."
This was no more than obligating the deponent to post
bond for his appearance at the examination. After all
testimony had been heard, the jury agreed upon a verdict,
delivered to the coroner by the foreman. The final detail was writing a summary of the examination, with the
coroner and every member of the jury affixing their signatures to the document. The body could then be interred
(or reinterred) and the records of the investigation
turned over to the county court. Later, the coroner collected his fee (133 pounds of tobacco) from the estate of
the deceased. If there was no estate, the county paid
the fee.[4]

If the coroner's jury decided that the deceased
had been a victim of murder, and the person accused of
the act had made his escape, the records of their inquest
were transmitted to the office of the secretary of the

---

4. Starke, Justice of Peace, pp. 106-110; Webb,
Justice of Peace, pp. 99-102; Hening, Statutes, V, 50,
340. Because of the requirement that the jury must view
the body, the coroner had the authority to exhume it any
time within fourteen days after burial. The decomposition
of the corpse prohibited a later exhumation. If the body
could not be placed in view of the coroner's jury, then
it was up to the county justices to determine the cause
of death.

colony. From this office was issued the necessary proclamation declaring the fugitive to be an outlaw. The
lands, goods and chattels of a person outlawed for a felony were forfeit to the crown, and "his Body at the King's
Disposal."[5]

There was always the possibility that the felon
was being pursued at the time of the inquest. Had there
been a witness to the crime, and had he rushed to the
nearest constable with his information, that officer could
raise hue and cry. The constable initiated this procedure
by requiring every man to take up the chase "by Horn and
by Voice." If the fugitive had already escaped the jurisdiction or precinct of the local officer, the constable
was to give notice to the next constable, and he to the
next, "'til the Offender is apprehended or pursued to the
Sea Side." Upon occasion, the governor issued a proclamation raising hue and cry upon a felon and offered a reward for his capture.[6]

---

5. Hening, Statutes, IV, 186; Webb, Justice of
Peace, pp. 103, 353.

6. Virginia Gazette, October 21, 1737, November 24,
1738; (Rind), July 6, 1769; Edmund Jenings to the Board
of Trade, April 24, 1710, PRO CO5/1317, Va. Col. Rec.
microfilm; Exec. Jour. Council Col. Va., V, 371. Hue and
cry was derived from the old hutesium et clamor, meaning

The pursuit of a felon bore resemblance to a game of hare and hounds. Sometimes the chase required the use of a Posse Comitatus, or "force of the county." Any available justice of the peace could call out every male in the county, freemen or servants, above the age of fifteen years and able to travel: only clergymen, the sick, the lame, and "impotent persons" were exempt. The justice was allowed his discretion in designating the number to be summoned and the manner in which they were to be armed. This posse was charged with pursuing, apprehending and bringing the wanted person or persons before the justice of the peace.[7]

Such strenuous methods were not always required. In many instances a warrant for the arrest of the accused was necessary; drawn up by a justice and executed by either the constable or the sheriff. An arrest could not be completed by words alone, for the arresting officer was required to physically lay his hands upon the accused. Force could be used and doors broken down, even without

---

to hoot (as with a horn), and cry. Hue and cry was also employed in the pursuit of runaway servants and slaves.

7. Webb, Justice of Peace, pp. 252-253.

a warrant, should the arresting officer be "refused quiet
Admittance." In civil cases such vigorous action was prohibited, but in the arrest of a felon "all private inconveniences must subside to publick Justice." Actually,
any man had the authority to arrest a felon without a
warrant, particularly if he had witnessed the act. A
justice of the peace could also direct a warrant to a
private citizen, but under these circumstances the individual would be under no obligations to execute it. Justices and other peace officers could naturally perform
an arrest for any offense to which they were a witness.[8]

Hunted criminals frequently escaped to neighbor-
ing colonies, primarily Maryland and North Carolina. In
1711 Governor Spotswood was complaining that "the Country
of North Carolina has long been the common Sanctuary of

---

8. Hening, Statutes, III, 292; Starke, Justice of
Peace, pp. 15-18. Some persons were immune from arrest
under certain circumstances. A member of the House of
Burgesses could not be arrested during, and ten days before and after, a meeting of the Assembly, except in
cases of treason, felony, or breach of the peace. A
witness summoned to testify at the General Court could
not be arrested upon any charge. He was allowed one
day's immunity for every twenty miles travelled. Militia going to and from musters, and when in actual service, were exempt from arrest in civil causes. (Hening
Statutes, III, 244, 299; VII, 100, 115.)

all our Runaway Servants and of all others that fly from
the due execution of the Laws in this and her Majesty's
other Plantations." During the seventeenth century, ex-
traditions from Maryland sometimes proved difficult, but
by the middle of the eighteenth this seems to have eased
considerably, and the available evidence indicates that
other colonies were equally cooperative in returning criminals to stand trial in Virginia. The only formality was
a request from the governor of Virginia addressed to the
governor of the colony in which the felon had sought his
freedom.[9]

On the other hand, the accused was quite often
placed under arrest before such steps became necessary.
The first step after his apprehension was the preliminary
hearing. It was the responsibility of the constable to

---

9. Spotswood to the Earl of Rochester, July 10, 1711,
R. A. Brock, ed., The Official Letters of Alexander
Spotswood, Lieutenant-Governor of the Colony of Virginia,
1710-1722 (Richmond, 1932-1935), I, 108; Virginia Gazette,
September 30, 1737; W. H. Brown and others, eds., The
Archives of Maryland (Baltimore, 1883-1919), XVII, 298ff,
385-386; XLV, 486-488; Exec. Jour. Council Col. Va., I,
67-68, 72-73, 284; III, 69, 142; Dinwiddie to ------,
May 20, 1752, PRO CO5/1338; and John Blair to Lewis
Burwell, May 20, 1751, PRO CO5/1338, Va. Col. Rec. micro-
film; Virginia Magazine of History and Biography, XVI
(July,1908), 75-76.

detain the alleged criminal as best he could until he could be brought before a justice for this hearing. If there was no gaol in the vicinity, the prisoner could be locked in the constable's home, put in irons, bound with ropes, or placed in the local stocks.[10]

For this preliminary hearing, the accused could be brought before any justice of the county court. Although he was not placed under oath, he was allowed to make a statement to be put into writing, and was required to place his signature or mark upon the document, especially if it was in the nature of a confession. Witnesses were heard and their depositions taken. If the justice then decided that this was a case that fell within the jurisdiction of the General Court, the prisoner was remanded to the county gaol. A warrant was issued to the local sheriff, requiring him to summon the county justices to an examining court to be held in the county courthouse, no less than five days nor more than ten days

---

10. Starke, Justice of Peace, p. 285; Webb, Justice of Peace, pp. 92, 93. In 1745 the sheriff of Augusta County was ordered to provide "shackels, bolts, handcuffs, and fetters of iron," for the safekeeping of a prisoner. (Virginia Historical Register, III [January, 1850], 14-15.)

after the date of the warrant. Even if the accused had

appeared innocent at the preliminary hearing, it was re-

quired that an examining court be held.[11]

The examining court, or "Called Court," was

peculiar to the judicial system of colonial Virginia.

As in the preliminary hearing, the prisoner was not

placed under oath, but was "brought to the barr" to an-

swer the charges against him. The initial procedure was

questioning by two or more justices.[12] Witnesses were

called, sworn and questioned by the bench. If their tes-

timony was pertinent to the case, they were placed under

a recognizance as surety for their appearance at the Gen-

eral Court or "the next Session of General Jail Delivery

of Criminals." The usual bond for witnesses was £10 or

£20, but upon occasion it ran as high as £40 or £50. The

---

11. Hening, Statutes, III, 390; Starke, Justice of Peace, pp. 114-121; Webb, Justice of Peace, pp. 109-115, 140.

12. The Act of 1705 that provided for these courts (Hening, Statutes, III, 389-392) did not specify the numbers of justices in attendance. One of them had to be of the quorum, and two signatures were required for the formal document committing the prisoner to the Williamsburg gaol. See Arthur P. Scott, Criminal Law in Colonial Virginia (Chicago, 1930), pp. 59ff.

accused was not without his rights, for it was his privilege to require the sheriff to summon witnesses who
might testify in his behalf. If, after all the testimony
had been heard, and the examining court was of the opinion that the accused should be tried before the General
Court in Williamsburg, he was returned to the local gaol.[13]

Conversely, if the examining court concluded
that the prisoner was innocent, his troubles were over,
for "The Power of Acquittal lodged with the Court is
absolute and conclusive." And not always was the accused
confined in prison until the next sitting of the General
Court. It was the responsibility of the county justices
to either commit the prisoner or admit him to bail. By
English common law the crimes of treason, murder, some
variations of manslaughter, counterfeiting and arson were
not bailable. Virginia statutes denied bail to blasphem-
ers, defamers of the governor or his appointees, ministers

13. York County Records, Orders and Judgments, 1720-
1729, pp. 24-25, 149, Virginia State Library, Richmond,
Virginia; ibid., 1746-1752; ibid., 1763-1765, p. 89; ibid.,
1774-1784, p. 153. If a witness was under twenty-one years
of age, he was legally considered an "infant" and his bond
was posted by his father or guardian. (Starke, Justice
of Peace, pp. 114-116; Charles Arthur Hoppin, "The Pulpit
Cloth of Appomattox Church," William and Mary Quarterly,
1st series, XXVII [July, 1918], 28-33.)

who violated the laws regulating marriages, free white
men or women who married Negroes or mulattoes and Roman
Catholics who refused to take the necessary oaths to the
government and then refused to deliver all arms and am-
munition to the nearest justice of the peace as required
by law. If, however, a prisoner was eligible for bail,
he was allowed twenty days to raise the money, during
which period he could not be removed to the public gaol
in Williamsburg.[14]

A prisoner not privileged to bail was returned
to the county gaol, there to be confined until he could
be transported to Williamsburg. Two of the justices
(one being of the quorum) prepared a mittimus committing
the accused to the care of the public gaoler in the
capital. To facilitate the journey, any two of the justices could prepare a precept empowering the sheriff to
impress, in any county through which he passed, men,
horses, or boats if he deemed them necessary for the
safe conveyance of his prisoner. Arriving in Williamsburg, the sheriff delivered his charge to the public

---

14. Starke, Justice of Peace, pp. 38-39, 115;
Hening, Statutes, III, 391.

gaoler before he notified the clerk of the General Court
of the committment and charge.[15]

There was one more legal process to be sustained
before the accused could be brought to trial before the
General Court--indictment by the grand jury. The grand
jury for the General Court was empanelled by the sheriff
of York County and was made up of twenty-four men then
in town. Although the relevant statute referred to them
as "by-standers," it was more stringent in specifying
that the jurors be freeholders and "of the most capable
persons." A different procedure was necessary for the
courts of oyer and terminer because these courts were
for the disposition of criminal cases only, and the number of freeholders then in Williamsburg was comparatively
small. Thus at least six days before the convening of
the court, the clerk of the General Court issued writs
to the sheriffs of York and James City Counties, requiring each to summon twelve freeholders from his county
to attend the sitting of the court. The lawmen were

---

15. Hening, Statutes, III, 390-391; Starke, Justice
of Peace, pp. 117-119. If a prisoner was particularly
dangerous, the public gaoler could impress additional
guards.

forced to exercise some caution in the selection of persons to serve as grand jurors. If, for instance, it was discovered that a person who was not a freeholder had served on the grand jury, those whom they had indicted were granted a pardon. The sheriff, or under-sheriff, responsible for the error was fined.[16]

The grand jury, after 1753, met on "Criminal Day," the sixth day after the convening of the General Court; for courts of oyer and terminer they sat the first day of the session. "Criminal Day" was not a day of trial for the defendant, but for his arraignment or indictment.[17] The jury was sworn after the appointment of

---

16. Hening, Statutes, V, 543; Webb, Justice of Peace, pp. 198-199; Exec. Jour. Council Col. Va., IV, 287; V, 37-38. A summoned juror who failed to appear was fined 400 pounds of tobacco. They could, however, have their fines remitted upon appealing to the Governor and Council and submitting a reasonable excuse. Among the excuses offered in these petitions were such reasonable alibis as never having been served with the summons, or ill health. The most unique occurred during the American Revolution when the industrious John Clark had his fine remitted because he "was busily making a coffin at the time he was summoned." (H. R. McIlwaine and Wilmer Hall, eds., Journals of the Council of the State of Virginia [Richmond, 1931-1952], III, 240.)

17. Virginia Gazette, October 21, 1737; Spotswood to the Lords of Trade, March 20, 1717/18, PRO CO5/1318, Va. Col. Rec. microfilm. Prior to 1748, the fourth day was designated as "Criminal Day." It seems that the original intent of the law was that criminals were to be

a foreman, followed by the governor's charge to the jury

in which he outlined their duties and responsibilities.

Of the few remaining extant copies of these charges,

those by Governor Dinwiddie are perhaps the most eloquent.

In October, 1755, he addressed the grand jury with these

words:

> You are here met and sworn to the dis-
> charge of a most necessary and essential Duty
> and of the greatest Importance y't can be
> placed in Man agreeable to our happy Constitu-
> tion. We have reason to dread y't our mani-
> fold Crimes and Iniquities have provok'd the
> Almighty God to punish us with the impend'g
> Prospect of Famine and the real Invasion of
> a barbarous and inhumane Enemy who delight
> in shed'g of Blood and the most unheard of
> Cruelties. Gent'n, The Laws are the Bulwarks
> of our most happy Constitut'n, but if those
> Laws are not put in due and proper Execut'n
> they become of no Effect, but rather an En-
> couragem't to the dissolute, profane and
> abandon'd Part of our People. I am heartily
> sorry to see so many Criminals now ready for
> tryal. It's Y'r Duty, Gent'n, with great
> Care, to Examine into the Facts for w'ch they
> are committed, and on proper Proofs to find
> the different Bills and present them to the

---

tried on these days. (Hening, _Statutes_, III, 293.) It
also appears that some grand jury proceedings were completed rather fast and there were some criminal trials
the same day. Jurors of the "vicinage" were ordered to
report to the General Court on the sixth day of the session, which suggests the possibility of their being called
upon that day. (Starke, _Justice of Peace_, p. 120.) Witnesses were also summoned to appear on the sixth day of
the General Court. (_Virginia Gazette_, October 24, 1751.)

> Court for their Tryal. From Y'r Known Under-
> stand'g and Knowledge, I doubt not of Y'r
> just discharge of the Trust repos'd in You,
> I therefore leave you to Your Examinat's and
> Enquiries.[18]

In courts of oyer and terminer, where the governor did

not sit as a judge, the charge was delivered by one of

the members of the Council.

The introductory formalities over, these "Twenty

four grave and substantial Men" then considered the bills

of indictment as drawn by the attorney-general, who also

presented the case for the king. Witnesses were called

and examined. The testimony of one witness was sufficient

to find a true bill in all criminal cases except treason;

two witnesses were necessary for this most heinous of all

---

18. R. A. Brock, ed., The Official Papers of Robert
Dinwiddie, Lieutenant-Governor of the Colony of Virginia,
1751-1758 (Richmond, 1933), II, 235. The disasters to
which Dinwiddie referred were the prospect of a terrible
drought in 1751, and the threat of an invasion by the
French. Other examples of Dinwiddie's charges to the
grand jury are in ibid., I, 32, 33, 34. The one on page
34 is particularly eloquent. Governor Gooch, on the
other hand, found himself ill-prepared to deliver such a
charge. Twice, within a five year interval, he wrote his
brother in England to send him a book containing this information, but to send it "sealed up." He complained
that he was forced to give these charges "out of my own
head." (William Gooch to Thomas Gooch, December 28, 1727,
September 4, 1732, Gooch typescripts, Colonial Williamsburg, Inc., 3-4, 33.)

charges. The grand jury, after examining the bills of indictment and hearing the testimony, either found a true bill by writing Billa vera, or found for the defendant by writing upon his indictment the word, Ignoramus. In the latter case the accused was immediately discharged. The docket for the court had been prepared earlier by the clerk, and cases were tried in the order in which they appeared.[19]

On the sixth day of the General Court and the second day of courts of oyer and terminer, the prisoners were brought to the bar of justice. The flag was hoisted to the top of the capitol flagstaff and the bell was rung to announce that the court was now in session.[20] Available evidence, admittedly scanty, suggests that criminal

19. Maude H. Woodfin and Marion Tinling, eds., Another Secret Diary of William Byrd of Westover, 1730-1741, With Letters & Literary Exercises, 1696-1725 (Richmond 1942) p. 118; Webb, Justice of Peace, pp. 193-195; Starke, Justice of Peace, pp. 214-215; Exec. Jour. Council Col. Va., III, 78; Virginia Gazette, May 15, 1746, April 17, 1752; (Rind), November 2, 1769.

20. This assumption is based upon only two references: the fact that Thomas Whitby petitioned for pay for his attendance "to hoyst the fflag this and last Assembly and Generall Court," (H. R. McIlwaine, ed., Journals of the House of Burgesses in Virginia, 1702-1712 [Richmond 1906-1915], p. 95 [hereafter cited as JHB plus date] and among the furnishings ordered for the capitol in June, 1722,

trials attracted more spectators than did civil proceedings. Certainly the courtroom was overcrowded at such
intriguing cases as that of a man charged with "killing
a woman after a new fashion." And William Byrd noticed
from his seat on the bench, the "abundance of women in
the gallery" when "a man was tried for ravishing a very
homely woman."[21]

The judges, following their attendance at
religious services for spiritual guidance, took their
place on the bench beneath Van Dyck's full-length portrait of Queen Anne.[22] The court crier then chanted the

---

was "a Bell for the use of the Assembly and General Court."
(Legis. Jour. Council Col. Va., II, 681.) Earlier, in
1697, and while the court was still sitting at Jamestown,
there is some evidence suggesting that a trumpeter may
have sounded the signal for the opening of the court.
(JHB 1695-1702, p. 111.)

21. Louis B. Wright and Marion Tinling, eds., The
Secret Diary of William Byrd of Westover, 1709-1712
(Richmond, 1941), pp. 95, 271. "Gallery" does not mean
only the balconies in the courtroom, but seems to include
other areas for spectators, "one at the Lower end of the
Room, and the other on the East side." (JHB 1702-1712,
pp. 29-30.)

22. Fred Shelley, ed., "The Journal of Ebenezer
Hazard in Virginia, 1777," Virginia Magazine of History
and Biography, LXI (October, 1954), 407. The church
attendance by the judges just prior to the trial is a
supposition on my part. It is possible that the chaplain
opened the sessions with a prayer, but all of the evidence,

traditional proclamation, "O Yes, O Yes, O Yes; silence

is commanded in the Court while his Majesties Governor

and Councell are sitting, upon paine of imprisonment."

Thus gaining the attention of the courtroom, he went on,

"All manner of persons that have any thing to doe at this

court draw neer and give your attendance and if any one

have any plaint to enter or suite to prosecute lett them

come forth and they shall be heard." Following this in-

vitation, the first case of the docket was called with,

"A B come forth and prosecute the action against C D or

else thou will be nonsuit." Then, with the appearance

of the plaintiff, or the attorney-general in criminal

cases, the crier summoned the defendant, "C D come forth

and save the and thy bayles or else though wilt forfeit

thy recognizance."[23]

---

admittedly weak, seems to indicate that he delivered the
sermon in church. In 1711 Byrd noted that "we were sworn
as judges of the Court of Oyer and Terminer and then we
went to church to hear the Commissary preach the sermon....
Then we returned to Court...." (Byrd, Secret Diary,
pp. 165, 452; Exec. Jour. Council Col. Va., IV, 398-399.)

23. This method of opening the General Court was
devised and passed into law in March, 1662, because of
the "want whereof many errors are committed the respect
due the courts soe neerly representing his royall majesties sacred person, by the clamorous unmannerlynes of
the people lost, and order, gravity and decorum which

Brought to the bar, the prisoner then heard the indictment against him read by the clerk, the first opportunity of the accused to hear the formal charges against him. He had been kept just as ignorant of the other facts of the case. He had not been allowed to see the panel of jurors called to try him, nor the list of witnesses summoned to testify, nor to examine the depositions taken at the preliminary hearings. Only in treason trials was the prisoner allowed this information. After the reading of the indictment, the defendant was asked how he pleaded, whether guilty or not guilty.[24]

---

should manifest the authority of a court in the court it selfe neglected." (Hening, Statutes, II, 58-60.) Inasmuch as there are no subsequent laws changing this form of opening the court, it can only be assumed that it was followed throughout the remainder of the colonial period. It may also be assumed that the words were sometimes changed to fit the nature of the case tried.

24. Webb, Justice of Peace, p. 238. Theoretically in English law a defendant could stand mute, that is, refuse to accept a jury trial and by implication demand a trial by ordeal in the old medieval manner. The crown then could order him subjected to Peine forte et dure to compel him to plead. Under this procedure he was crushed to death by weights placed on top of him. The advantage was that if he died before he accepted a trial, he would not have been convicted as a felon and his estate would not be forfeited to the crown. The question is academic for colonial Virginia, for there is no record of the procedure ever having been used. The one source that held

By the middle of the eighteenth century the
defendant was permitted advice of counsel if he could
afford such services. Although it appears that criminals sometimes employed attorneys as early as 1711, it
was not until 1734 that a statute was placed upon the
books stating "That in all trials for capital offences,
the prisoner, upon his petition to the court, shall be
allowed counsel." There are few instances on record
suggesting that felons availed themselves of the services of lawyers. The majority of those tried for capital offences usually fell into the lower economic
brackets and therefore could assure no lawyer the payment of a fee. In those rare instances when a counsel
for the defendant is mentioned, there was a reasonable
doubt as to the guilt of the client, and the attorney
apparently felt that he could clear the accused and,

---

it even was applicable to the colony was Starke, Justice
of Peace, p. 257. He erred, however, in stating that the
goods of the victim reverted to the crown. In addition,
the procedure had been abolished in England just about
the time Starke was writing. (Theodore F. T. Plucknett,
A Concise History of the Common Law, 5th ed. [Boston,
1956], p. 126.)

incidentally, collect his fee.[25]

A counsel for the defense was, in the main, more of a luxury than a necessity, and the trial proceeded whether or not the prisoner had been able to secure legal aid. Following the plea by the accused, the petit jury was empaneled. The right to trial by jury was felt to be an inherent prerogative of every Englishman, "being contemporary with the Foundations of the State, and one of the Pillars of it, both as to Age and Consequence."[26]

The venire of the petit jury was not composed of by-standers as had been the grand jury, but had been summoned by the sheriff as a result of a writ issued by the clerk when the prisoner had first been delivered to

---

25. Spotswood to the Council of Trade, March 6, 1711, Brock, Spotswood Letters, I, 57; Hening, Statutes, IV, 404; Webb, Justice of Peace, p. 114; Virginia Gazette, October 14, 1737; (Rind), April 22, 1773.

26. Starke, Justice of Peace, p. 233. By 1642, and possibly even earlier, Virginians had been assured of the right of trial by jury. In that year, the Assembly, in a document entitled "The Declaration against the Company to be entered as the twenty first act," stated "the legal trial per juries in all criminal and civil causes where it shall be demanded." (Hening, Statutes, I, 231.)

gaol. The law required that they be freeholders living

in the "vicinage" of the spot where the crime was alleged

to have been committed.[27] Certain qualifications were

necessary for a juror. First, he had to be a freeholder

with real and personal holdings to the value of £100

current money.[28] Any person who was summoned and then

refused to serve was liable to a fine of 400 pounds of

tobacco. If jurors were unavoidably detained, or were

challenged, the sheriff was allowed to meet the requi-

site number by empanelling the "good and lawful free-

holders of the by standers." These replacements could

be summoned from any part of, and within a one-half mile

radius of, the City of Williamsburg.[29] With the westward

---

27. Hening, Statutes, IV, 404. The petit jury for
a felony trial was sometimes referred to as "the Jury of
Life and Death." (Webb, Justice of Peace, p. 193.)

28. Hening, Statutes, III, 176; V, 525-526. Originally this was sterling value. Jurors in the county
courts were required to have assets to the value of £50
current money. No exception to the value of a freeholder's
property could be made unless they were specified before
the juror was sworn. (Ibid., IV, 405.)

29. Hening, Statutes, III, 211; IV, 404-405; VI,
349-350. In trials other than felony or treason, juries
were summoned from Williamsburg and vicinity. (Ibid., V,
525.) If a sheriff or under-sheriff summoned as a petit
juror any person who was not a freeholder, that official
was liable to a fine. (Exec. Jour. Council Col. Va., IV,

expansion of the colony of Virginia, the long journey
to Williamsburg increasingly imposed a hardship upon
those summoned as jurors, despite the travel allowance
granted them for their pains. Convicts sent from England to the colony as indentured servants and who then
found themselves accused of a felony, were granted a
jury trial, but after 1738 the petit jury was made up
entirely of by-standers.[30]

Before the jury was sworn, the defense had
the opportunity to challenge the prospective jurors.
The accused was allowed any number of challenges for
cause, including: not owning an estate of sufficient
value, conviction of some crime in the past, and

287.) Those ineligible for jury duty included aliens,
foreigners not yet naturalized, apothecaries, persons indicted, attainted or outlawed, conspirators, clergymen,
infants under fourteen years, and the public gaoler.
(Webb, Justice of Peace, p. 196.)

30. Hening, Statutes, I, 313; V, 25. The inconven-
ience of the long journey to Williamsburg was one of the
reasons given in 1749 for the introduction of a bill pro-
posing the removal of the capital from Williamsburg to
New Castle. (Legis. Jour. Council Col. Va., II, 1037.)
The long journey made by many jurors was also listed as
one of the objections in 1773 when a bill was introduced
to provide circuit courts in the colony. The bill failed
only because the Assembly could not agree upon a salary
for the judges. (Dunmore to Dartmouth, March 18, 1774,
Strachey Papers, Clements Library, Ann Arbor, Michigan.)

"Partiality." This latter embraced such objections as malice, favor, a previously expressed opinion, or kinship with a litigant or member of the court. If a challenge was made on the grounds of "Partiality," the court appointed and swore in two of the panel as "Triers," whose duty it was to evaluate and determine the validity of the challenge. In addition, the prisoner was allowed twenty peremptory challenges, except in cases of treason or petit treason where the accused was allowed as many as thirty-five peremptory challenges without penalty. If, however, he exceeded this number of peremptory challenges, he was immediately adjudged guilty without the formality of a trial and sentenced to be hanged. And prisoners did exercise their right to challenge in the eighteenth century. In 1737, Daniel Handley, indicted for robbery, "excepted against all the Venire but one." In this instance Handley's challenges were but prolonging his apprehension, for another jury was quickly assembled from the by-standers, who just as quickly found him guilty. In all instances, those jurors removed from the original panel by a successful challenge were replaced

by freeholders from among the by-standers, or from the
community.[31]

With the membership of the jury agreed upon,
a foreman was selected and sworn to an oath that the
verdict would be "according to the best of yor cunning."
The remainder of the jury were then sworn. Having taken
the oath, a juror from this time on was not allowed to
leave the courtroom without the permission of the court,
and even then the law required that an officer of the
court accompany him, "So cautious is the Law to prevent
all sinister Practice in the Trial of Causes."[32]

---

31.   Webb, Justice of Peace, pp. 196-197; Hening,
Statutes, IV, 271, 404-405; Virginia Gazette, October 21,
1737. A juror was sometimes able to disqualify himself.
Colonel Charles Carter, in 1751, refused in open court
to serve on a jury. Although the source states no reason, one might speculate that the Colonel, as a member
of the House of Burgesses, felt that he was on the same
level as a Peer of the realm, and under English common
law a Peer could challenge himself if neither party did.
("Diary of John Blair," William and Mary Quarterly, 1st
series, VII (January, 1899), 139; Webb, Justice of Peace,
p. 196.)

32.   "Acts, Orders and Resolutions of the General
Assembly of Virginia, at Sessions of March 1643-1646,"
Virginia Magazine of History and Biography, XXIII (July,
1915), 226-227; Webb, Justice of Peace, p. 198.

Not until then did the actual trial get under-
way with the presentation of the charge by the prosecution. In most criminal cases, the burden of proof rested
with the king's attorney. There were some exceptions,
notably those crimes in which the detection of guilt was
difficult. This was true in indictments involving the
murder of illegitimate children by the mother, or the
killing of deer out of season. In such cases, the burden of proof was shifted to the defendant.[33]

On the morning of the trial, the witnesses
subpoenaed to testify against the alleged felon met with
the attorney-general "to instruct him in forming Indictments against the Criminals." The depositions made by
these witnesses at the preliminary hearing were used by
the prosecution in the presentation of the case, but
these alone were not sufficient to win a conviction. It
was necessary that a witness appear in person to present
oral testimony. A witness who failed to answer to his
name when first called forfeited those allowances granted

---

33. Starke, _Justice of Peace_, p. 154; Hening,
Statutes, III, 516; V, 62. A person was allowed to kill
a deer out of season if he needed the meat for food. But
if he was apprehended, it was up to the hunter to prove
his need.

him by law. Only in those instances where the witness had died, or had some lawful reason for his absence, were the depositions, without corroborating oral testimony, admitted as evidence.[34]

Subpoenas had been issued to the designated witnesses on the day the sheriff had delivered the prisoner to Williamsburg. Summons as a witness carried some privileges with it. Writs and processes could not be served on him while he was coming, attending, or returning from court. For every mile that the witness travelled, he was paid one and one-half pounds of tobacco. For every day his presence was required in court, he was allowed sixty pounds of tobacco. Because witnesses were often paid by the government, it was felt that a maximum of three witnesses was enough to verify any criminal charge. On the other hand, the testimony of

---

34. Virginia Gazette, October 24, 1751; Hening, Statutes, III, 299; Starke, Justice of Peace, pp. 119-120, 149. Witnesses pleading "sickness, age or other lawful disability," which made them incapable of attending court, were required to secure a certificate from a justice of the peace stating the nature of their disability. (Hening, Statutes, III, 297.)

at least two witnesses was considered necessary to prove
a felony.[35]

Insofar as age was concerned, a wide latitude
was allowed in qualifying a witness. A person was considered to be "of the Age of Discretion" at fourteen
years. A child younger than fourteen was allowed as a
witness "if it appear he hath a competent Discretion."[36]
On the other hand, certain individuals were disqualified
as witnesses. A convicted felon was ineligible unless
he had been granted a pardon or had been extended benefit
of clergy. A wife could not be forced to testify against
her husband, or a husband against his wife, unless the

---

35. Hening, Statutes, VI, 338; Webb, Justice of
Peace, p. 136; Starke, Justice of Peace, p. 157.

36. Starke, Justice of Peace, p. 145. Children
under fourteen could testify against their parents in
cases involving witchcraft. A married woman or an
"infant" under fourteen could not enter into a recognizance, but had to find surety (a person acting as
guarantor, who would be liable in the event of default).
If they could not furnish surety, they were to be committed to gaol until the time of the trial. The reasoning behind this was that a married woman was a Feme
Covert, "that is, under her Husband's Power, and therefore disabled to make any Bargain, or Contract without
his Consent, Privity, Allowance, or Confirmation; she
can neither sue, or be sued, without her Husband...."
(Webb, Justice of Peace, pp. 135, 137, 152, 265.)

charge was treason.[37] A "Popish Recusant Convict" was
denied the privilege of being a witness. Negroes,
mulattoes and Indians, free or slave, were not allowed
to give evidence except against other Negroes, mulattoes
or Indians. After 1748 convicts could testify only
against other convicts. This restriction was considered
necessary as it was generally assumed they were "commonly
of such base and corrupt principles, that their testimony cannot be depended upon."[38]

There were sometimes strange deviations from
the norm in the presentation of evidence. A juror, or
even a judge, could testify against the accused in open
court and in the very case on which they were serving,

---

37. There were some exceptions to these provisions,
including a forced marriage, or in cases where husband
and wife had cause to demand sureties of the peace against
each other. (Webb, Justice of Peace, p. 135; Starke,
Justice of Peace, p. 145.)

38. Hening, Statutes, V, 546-547; Webb, Justice of
Peace, p. 137; Starke, Justice of Peace, p. 148. A
"Popish Recusant" was a Roman Catholic. He became a convict when he was found guilty of an indictment or when he
refused to take the oaths of allegiance, supremacy, or
abjuration, and refused to take the Protestant sacrament.
These latter denials were entered as convictions. Starke,
in 1774, noted, "As we have happily very few Papists in
this Colony, there is no Occasion to be more particular
under this Title, which perhaps·may have been wholly
omitted." (Starke, Justice of Peace, p. 294.)

although there is no evidence that this ever happened.
It was not unknown for a confessed felon, upon an implied promise of leniency, to turn king's evidence and
testify against those who had but recently been his com-
patriots.[39]

By no means was the privilege of calling witnesses limited to the prosecution. A defendant could
require the sheriff to summon persons to testify in his
behalf. A witness, before he could take the stand, first
had to be sworn.[40] A witness for the prosecution, or
king's witness, was not allowed to be cross-examined until he had first given his testimony for the crown, but
he had to be examined in the presence of the accused.
He was not allowed to read his deposition made during

---

39. Virginia Gazette, October 21, 1737; Webb, Justice
of Peace, p. 135; Starke, Justice of Peace, pp. 144, 146.
Patrick Gibling, who turned king's evidence against Daniel
Handley, was tried in the General Court one year later.
This, presumably, was for the same crime that Handley had
been convicted. Gibling was also found guilty, but did
not receive the death sentence as had Handley, but was
burnt in the hand, perhaps his reward for turning king's
evidence in the earlier trial. (Virginia Gazette, November 3, 1738.)

40. Starke, Justice of Peace, p. 141. Quakers were
allowed to "Affirm" in civil cases, but could not be admitted as witnesses in criminal trials unless they had
been sworn. (Webb, Justice of Peace, p. 137; Starke,
Justice of Peace, p. 147.)

the preliminary hearing, albeit he was allowed the use
of notes "to refresh his Memory." Depositions were admitted as evidence only when the witness was dead, too
ill to come to court, or could not be found, "for whilst
the Witness is living they [depositions] are not the best
Evidence the Nature of the Thing will admit of...." Hear-
say evidence was not admissible, although the dying statement of a murdered man was considered valid. And there
were instances in which conviction was obtained on what
could be considered circumstantial evidence.[41]

In addition to the questions put to the witness
by the prosecution and the judges, the court could "in-
dulge" the prisoner, or his counsel, to interrogate the
testifier. Under these circumstances, questions could
be so phrased as to either discredit the testimony of the
witness or place a more favorable construction upon it.
Testimony could be invalidated if the defense could prove
that the witness was lying, and such proof was often followed by a motion by the defense counsel calling for an
indictment of the witness for perjury. One method of

---

41. Starke, Justice of Peace, pp. 144, 149;
Virginia Gazette, May 26 and June 16, 1768.

discrediting a witness was to demonstrate variations between his original deposition and his testimony at the
trial, and among the rights of the prisoner during the
trial was to request a reading of the original deposition.[42]

The trial neared its end with the testimony of
the last witness. It seems likely, though by no means
certain, that the prisoner was given one last opportunity
to make a plea for his life. Certainly the prosecution
delivered a summing-up of the case. This concluded, the
charge to the jury was made by the presiding judge.[43]

The jury was now isolated in a room "without
Meat, Drink, Fire, or Candle, 'til they are agreed of

---

42. Starke, Justice of Peace, p. 147; Virginia
Gazette (Purdie & Dixon), April 22, 1773. A prisoner did
not have the right to demand the opportunity to examine
"the witness apart," but it was usually granted upon his
request to the court.

43. Robert Beverley, The History and Present State
of Virginia, ed. by Louis B. Wright (Chapel Hill, 1947),
p. 110. If the House of Burgesses was in session, there
were sometimes frequent interruptions in the General
Court. The sergeant at arms would enter the courtroom
with the mace in his arms and summon those Burgesses engaged in court business to return to the House. (JHB,
1752-1758, pp. 328, 397.) In 1768 the governor prorogued
the House of Burgesses because they "trespassed so much
on the General Court, by obstructing all business there
for several days." (JHB, 1766-1769, p. 177.)

their Verdict." They were allowed to communicate with no one other than the sheriff or under-sheriff standing guard outside the door, and then only if they had decided the case. They were prohibited from requesting a witness to repeat the testimony he had given in the courtroom. Should this be done, the verdict was set aside and the responsible jurors charged with a misdemeanor. A similar charge was lodged against them if they cast lots in reaching a decision. A jury was subject to severe penalties if they arrived at a verdict contrary to the evidence presented at the trial. If they ate or drank at the expense of the party for whom the verdict was found, the verdict was set aside and the jurors fined. If they ate or drank at their own expense, they were only fined and the verdict allowed to stand.[44] Because of the refusal to discharge a jury until it arrived at a verdict, there were no hung juries in colonial Virginia.

Their decision made, the jurors were escorted back into the courtroom by the officer watching over them. The verdict had to be given in open court. The accused was brought to the bar, and the jury commanded to look

---

44. Webb, Justice of Peace, pp. 197-198; Hening, Statutes, I, 314, II, 74.

upon him as the foreman made known their decision. The law demanded that the verdict be legally perfect, although the original indictment could be lessened by the jury. For instance, in a murder case they might find the accused guilty, but they could change the charge to manslaughter, chance-medley or self-defense. Before a verdict became an acceptable legal document, the foreman was required to affix his signature.[45]

The final step in a felony trial was the pronouncement of the sentence upon the convicted felon. This was not done at the conclusion of the trial, for it seems that all criminals convicted during any one session were brought into the court and sentenced on the same day, presumably the last day of the session.[46] The prisoners were brought before the bar and there asked by the presiding judge if they had anything to say. Some did. In 1751 an old offender by the name

45. Webb, Justice of Peace, pp. 352-353. Chance-medley was killing another without malice or intent.

46. This assumption is based on a study of the sentencing of criminals as reported in the Virginia Gazette, which sometimes used the phrase, "This Day the Criminals who were convicted at the Beginning of this General Court, were brought to the Bar, to receive their Sentence...." (Virginia Gazette, November 3, 1738.)

of Thomas Seale "made a Petition to the Court, before

Sentence was passed, desiring their Honours Clemency;

alledging, That tho' a Brother should sin Seventy Times

Seven, yet, on his Repentance, Christianity obliged us

to forgive him." This colorful plea availed him little,

and he was sentenced to hang.[47]

     There were several other pleas a convicted

criminal might make before judgment was passed upon him

or her. A pregnant female could "plead her belly." Un-

der such circumstances a "jury of matrons" was empanelled

to determine if she was really "quick with child." If

they reported her claim valid, the verdict was respited

until after the birth of the child.[48]

---

     47. Virginia Gazette, May 9, 1751. This conviction
was for horse-stealing. It was the fourth occasion that
Seale had been brought before the General Court. He had
been convicted once before but had been pardoned. (Ibid.,
April 18, 1751.) In 1749 he had been convicted of robbing
a house in Norfolk. While confined in the Norfolk gaol,
he had escaped through the chimney of the prison, robbed
the same house a second time, and returned to prison to
cast suspicion from him. (Maryland Gazette, July 26, 1749;
Pennsylvania Gazette, August 3, 1749.) Upon the occasion
mentioned above,his eloquent plea apparently impressed
someone, for at "the earnest Solicitation of several
Gentlemen of Distinction," he was once again pardoned by
the Governor. (Virginia Gazette, August 16, 1751.)

     48. Byrd, Secret Diary, pp. 452-453.

Under some circumstances, a convicted person had recourse to still another plea in an effort to escape the supreme punishment: the privilege of claiming benefit of clergy. This holdover from medieval times could be claimed if the prisoner had not been convicted of willful murder, rape, treason, arson, horse-stealing, burglary or robbery. Originally, this privilege had been based on the premise of protecting the better-educated English clergy from the vengeance of the temporal courts. Thus, to show himself entitled, the prisoner was required to demonstrate his ability by reading a passage from the Bible. If customary English usage was followed, the clerk turned to the fifty-first Psalm with its opening lines, "Have mercy upon me, O God, according to thy loving kindness; according unto the multitude of thy tender mercies blot out my transgressions." Upon the successful reading of the passage, the prisoner was granted his clergy and became a "clerk convict."[49]

---

49. Starke, Justice of Peace, pp. 89-90; George W. Dalzell, Benefit of Clergy in America and Related Matters (Winston-Salem, 1955), p. 24. The value set upon reading in medieval England was explained by Webb in these words: "It was a Privilege to save the Life of a Criminal, if he was a Man of Learning, that is, if he could read; for, as such, he might be useful to the Public, he declaring, that

The year 1732 saw an expansion in the Virginia statute relating to benefit of clergy. It no longer remained an exclusive preserve for males; women were now allowed to petition for the right. This same statute was responsible for one other radical change--the elimination of the reading requirement. Henceforth any eligible person convicted under a clergyable crime need only petition to receive benefit of clergy "as if he had read as a clerk."[50]

Bestowing clergy did not mean that the petitioner got off scot-free. As soon as the convicted felon was granted the privilege, the public gaoler "in open

---

he had vowed, or was resolved to enter into Religious Orders, and that the Reading was to shew that he was qualified." (Webb, Justice of Peace, p. 82.) "A man found guilty of felony...and praying his clergy, and thereupon reading as a clerke...is called a clerk convict." (Oxford English Dictionary, II, 493.)

50. Hening, Statutes, IV, 326; V, 546. At this time, Negroes, mulattoes and Indians were extended benefit of clergy, with the following exceptions: manslaughter, breaking and entering either in the night or day and taking away goods to the value of five shillings sterling. There were occasions, prior to 1732, that a modified form of benefit of clergy was granted. In 1701, three criminals, found guilty of manslaughter and robbery, prayed for the clemency of the court, but confessed they could not read. They were transported out of the colony. (Two Year List of General Court Trials, November, 1701, PRO CO5/1312, Va. Col. Rec. microfilm.)

Court" branded that person on the "Brawn of the left

Thumb." If the prisoner had been convicted of a hom-

icide other than willful murder (manslaughter, self-

defense, chance-medley, etc.), he was branded with the

letter M. For all other felonies the letter T was cus-

tomary. A person was allowed benefit of clergy only one

time, the brand thereafter serving as an identifying

mark. The clerk of the court was also required to make

a record of the fact. It was not unknown for a prisoner

who was granted his clergy to receive an additional term.

In any event, the granting of benefit of clergy restored

all citizenship rights to the petitioner.[51]

The application of the branding iron did not

always result in a disfiguring or identifying scar. As

early as 1739 there is the record of one John Oldham

who, convicted of manslaughter, was "burnt in the Hand

---

51. Starke, Justice of Peace, pp. 87-88, 91; Virginia Gazette (Purdie & Dixon), May 9, 1771; (Rind),
May 9, 1771. In June, 1751, Anthony Weathered was convicted of a felony, and having received benefit of
clergy the preceding December under an alias, was refused clergy a second time and sentenced to die. Earlier, in 1738, Elizabeth Blair had pleaded "the Benefit
of the Act," but she had already received her clergy in
an earlier conviction and was refused clemency a second
time. (Virginia Gazette [Purdie & Dixon], May 9, 1771;
Boston Gazette, May 29, 1738.)

with a cold iron."[52] By 1774 this seems to have been

the habitual practice, for Richard Starke in his *Justice*

of the Peace commented:

> And therefore the burning in the Hand
> seems to be of little Use, and...can scarcely
> be called even so much as a slight Punishment,
> but rather a Piece of absurd Pageantry, tend-
> ing neither to the Reformation of the Offender,
> nor for Example to others; to wit, burning the
> Offender in the Hand with an Iron scarcely
> heated.[53]

There was still one legal maneuver open to the

prisoner convicted of a non-clergyable crime. An arrest

of judgment could be obtained and a new trial ordered if

he could prove there had been a technical error in pro-

cedure. There is, however, little evidence that prisoners

ever employed this expedient, presumably because they

customarily pleaded their own cases and were seldom skilled

in the niceties of the law.[54]

---

52. *Virginia Gazette*, December 14, 1739. The very
fact that this was noted rather than the usual "Burnt in
the Hand" indicates that the application of a cold iron
was unusual at this date.

53. Starke, *Justice of Peace*, p. 88. Benefit of
clergy was not abolished in Virginia until 1796 and was
not completely abolished in England until 1827.

54. R. T. Barton, ed., *Virginia Colonial Decisions:
The Reports by Sir John Randolph and by Edward Barradall
of Decisions of the General Court of Virginia, 1728-1741*

If the convicted felon was unable to take legal recourse to any of these possibilities, he stood at the bar of the General Court while the governor or presiding judge delivered the sentence. Every sentence, it seems, was read from a previously prepared document.[55]

Hope was not to be completely abandoned after the criminal had heard his doom pronounced--he might sue for a pardon under any one of three procedures. Convicted of homicide by misadventure or in self-defense, he was eligible for a "pardon of course" by merely undergoing the formalities of suing "out his Pardon."[56] A "pardon of grace" could be granted by the governor to all convicted felons with the exception of murderers and traitors. Since pardon was an executive function, the

---

(Boston, 1909), II, B50. There was an arrest of judgment granted in the October, 1735, court when the attorney for an unnamed horse thief proved that the venire facias summoning the jury to try him was issued in the wrong county.

55. William Gooch to Thomas Gooch, February 18, 1727, Gooch typescripts, Colonial Williamsburg, Inc.; John Blair to Lewis Burwell, May 20, 1751, PRO CO5/1338, Va. Col. Rec. microfilm.

56. Webb, Justice of Peace, pp. 245-246. Examples of this procedure are unusual, because the examining court likely would have found the homicide justifiable and there would have been no trial. And if the case had come to trial, the jury probably would have brought in a verdict of not guilty.

governor exercised his power of mercy in consultation
with his Council. Usually, it was initiated through a
petition submitted by friends and neighbors of the convicted person, requesting a careful review of the circumstances of the crime or the trial. Upon occasion,
it was the councillors themselves who requested executive clemency. And because of the peculiar judicial
system, the councillors sometimes found themselves re-
viewing the trial which they had conducted. Pardons
were sometimes granted on a conditional basis. In one
such case, pardon was promised a fugitive horse thief
if he delivered himself to the General Court. As late
as 1734 it was an occasional practice to grant a criminal a pardon on the condition that he be transported
out of the colony "into some other of his Majesties
Plantations for the Term of Seven Years." Two men convicted of stealing slaves and horses in 1772 were
granted pardons with the proviso that they enlist in
the crew of one of the ships of His Majesty's Navy.
Extenuating circumstances sometimes precipitated amnesty.
Such was the case of one Sharper, "a great runaway and
rogue," who received the pardon of the governor in 1751

in order "to avoid some difficulty as to regularity."[57]

Occasionally a governor might emulate British royal precedent and celebrate his arrival in the colony by pardoning the first felon convicted in his term of office. In a like manner, a rather notorious pirate, John Vidal, was granted clemency in 1727 to mark both the accession of King George II and the arrival of Governor William Gooch in Virginia. A "pardon of grace," for a non-clergyable offence, had to be personally plead by the applicant. Traditional procedure required the condemned man to station himself in the middle of the bar in the General Court Room, there to fall upon his knees and make his plea in a position of supplication. The governor, in the company of the Council, would then consider the merits of the petition. If the pardon was

---

57. Council Journals, 1771, PRO CO5/1349, Va. Col. Rec. microfilm; Exec. Jour. Council Col. Va., I, 397; II, 133; III, 128, 163; IV, xxi, 31, 70, 92, 206, 213, 249; V, 220, 339; Scott, Criminal Law, pp. 116-117; Virginia Magazine of History and Biography, XIX (July, 1911), 263-264; Virginia Gazette (Purdie & Dixon), June 11, 1772. Upon one occasion a criminal's pardon was entered into the records although he was dead. Upon another, the Governor and Council decided "to pardon the punishment of burning in the hand." (Exec. Jour. Council Col. Va., III, 288; IV, xxi.) Under English law a person could be reprieved or pardoned if "thought fit to serve the King in his Army, or Navy...." (Webb, Justice of Peace, p. 246.)

allowed, the attorney-general was instructed to prepare the document for the signature of the governor.[58]

Conviction for willful murder or treason was something else. Under these circumstances, the governor could only reprieve until "the King's Pleasure be Known." Should the Council decide that the condemned was "a fitt Object of Mercy," the governor wrote to the secretary of state, and later to the Board of Trade, stating the bare facts of the case and requesting that an intercession be made to the king on behalf of the person under sentence. Sometimes he justified his intercession on the grounds that the court had felt the verdict of the jury to be unjust.[59] This was the explanation in the case of Andrew Bourne, an overseer who had killed a slave in a fit of passion, yet had been convicted by the jury of willful murder. In requesting clemency for Bourne, Governor

---

58. "Diary of John Blair," William and Mary Quarterly, 1st series, VIII (July, 1899), 9; September 12, 1727, "Virginia Council Journals," Virginia Magazine of History and Biography, XXXII (July, 1924), pp. 242-243; Webb, Justice of Peace, p. 245; Exec. Jour. Council Col. Va., III, 288; IV, xxi; Scott, Criminal Law, pp. 117-118, 229n.

59. Dartmouth to George III, October 1, 1765, PRO CO5/1345; and Fauquier to the Board of Trade, August 1, 1765, ibid., Va. Col. Rec. microfilm; Virginia Gazette, November 24, 1738.

Gooch noted,

> the executing of him for this offence may
> make the slaves very insolent, and give
> them occasion to contemn their Masters &
> overseers, which may be of dangerous Con-
> sequences in a Country where the negroes
> are so numerous and make the most valuable
> part of the People's Estates.[60]

But if a malefactor had been convicted of an
unclergyable crime, and the Council "were of opinion that
he was too atrocious an offender to be recommended for a
pardon," he had reached the end of his road. The death
warrant, prepared by the attorney-general, was signed
by the governor in the presence of the Council. The punishment for felony was four-fold. The greatest personal
loss was, of course, the loss of life. But the felon
also suffered "Corruption of Blood, so as he hath neither
Ancestor, Heir, nor Posterity." His estate, both goods
and lands, was forfeited to the crown.[61]

---

60. Gooch to the Secretary of State, June 29, 1729,
PRO CO5/1337, Va. Col. Rec. microfilm. In 1770, the
Council recommended a pardon for the murderer, Moses Riggs,
on the grounds that he was insane. (Council Journal, 1770,
PRO CO5/1349, Va. Col. Rec. microfilm.)

61. Council Journal, June 11, 1771, PRO CO5/1349,
Va. Col. Rec. microfilm; "Diary of John Blair," William
and Mary Quarterly, 1st series, VIII (July, 1899), 8;
Exec. Jour. Council Col. Va., II, 236; III, 179; Webb,
Justice of Peace, p. 148; Starke, Justice of Peace,
pp. 174-176.

The day of execution was designated in the death warrant, the law requiring at least a ten day interval between the signing of the death warrant and the day of performance. Once the governor had placed his signature on the death warrant, the only recourse left to the condemned man was his own ingenuity. John Sparks, sentenced to death in 1752, adopted desperate and novel measures to insure his own "gaol delivery." As were all prisoners awaiting the gallows, Sparks was heavily ironed and watched by a special guard who had been impressed to provide maximum security. Nevertheless, this bold fellow somehow managed to saw his irons, and when the gaoler opened the cell door, Sparks hit him in the head with a bottle and escaped. His daring escapade availed him little; in fact, it hastened his demise. He was apprehended on a Thursday and, to prevent a recurrence of his escape, was hanged on Friday.[62]

---

62. Virginia Gazette, July 3, 1752. John Sparks appears to have been an habitual criminal. Earlier this same year the king had remitted a fine of £25, imposed upon Sparks for attempted highway robbery. This had been a concession to the "unhappy Circumstances of his Family," and because he was "a Youth under Age." (Holderness to the Lords of Trade, March 26, 1752, PRO CO5/1327, Va. Col. Rec. microfilm.) In 1768, four prisoners sawed off their irons, attacked the guard with iron bars, and made their

The condemned criminal, assuming the gaoler was able to keep him in confinement, was prepared both spiritually and physically for the day of his death. Frequent visits by the chaplain supposedly prepared him to meet his Maker. No doubt this spiritual preparation was somewhat enhanced in 1772 when Peter Pelham, not only the gaoler, but also the organist for Bruton Parish Church, was required to carry all condemned prisoners to church every Sunday. This, however, appears not to have been the result of any great concern for the spiritual welfare of the prisoners, but rather to prevent their escape while the gaoler was absent. To make certain the criminal appeared in the best of health on the day he was to die, a physician was summoned whenever he manifested signs of indisposition.[63]

---

escape. They were "briskly pursued," and apprehended. (Virginia Gazette [Rind], August 25, 1768.) Although it was required that a slave convicted of a felony not be executed for a period of ten days (Hening, Statutes, VI, 106), this was not always the case. One incident of speedy justice occurred in 1751 in the James City County Court when John Blair noted in his diary, "a felony comtd last nt, the felon tried, sentenced and executd this afternoon." (William and Mary Quarterly, 1st series, VIII [July, 1899], 12.)

63. Exec. Jour. Council Col. Va., V, 373; JHB 1712-1716, pp. 95, 223; William A. R. Goodwin, The Record of Bruton Parish Church, ed. by Mary Goodwin (Richmond, 1941), p.41.

Inclement weather was no bar to an execution.
Around noon of the day specified in the death warrant,
the prisoner was taken from the gaol. Placed on a cart,
or sometimes a sledge, and attended by a clergyman, he
was drawn to "the public gallows, near this city." The
sheriff, in his capacity as public hangman, was waiting.
The cart was drawn beneath the gallows. The condemned
person was then allowed his last words. Many seemed
"penitent," and died with a "Composure of Mind." Others
took this opportunity to confess their crimes, as did
Jonathan Faithful in 1740, who then "declar'd he was in
Charity with all Mankind, and desir'd others to take
Warning by his unhappy Example."[64] Equally eloquent
were the last remarks of colonial Virginia's most famous counterfeiter, who:

> addressed himself to the Spectators, in a
> very moving and pathetic Speech on the fatal
> Consequences attending an early Habit of
> Vice, which had been the Means of bringing
> him to that shameful and untimely End. He

---

64. "Diary of John Blair," William and Mary Quarterly, 1st series, VII (January, 1899), 149; Virginia
Gazette, January 4, 1740; (Rind) June 1, 1769. Accounts
of hangings in the Maryland Gazette indicate that executions in the colony of Maryland were performed near the
spot of the crime. After death, the corpse was taken
to the nearest roadside and there hanged in chains.
This was particularly true of Negroes who were hanged.

appeared with a Composure of Mind, not frequently attending Men in his unhappy Circumstances, and died in a very penitent
Manner.[65]

With the completion of these final words, the

doomed man, noose snug around his neck, was "turn'd off"

the cart. Death was not always instant. For instance,

there was Anthony Francis Dittond, the confessed murderer

of Mr. Evans, the coachmaker. Dittond was a "lusty Man"

and did not take to dying too readily. He still strug-

gled after two or three minutes of swinging at the end

of the rope. The executioner then grasped his legs and

bore down to strangle him "and put him out of his Pain

the sooner." Under the combined weight of the dying man

and his executioner, the rope parted and Dittond fell

senseless to the ground. For a short period he lay mo-

tionless, then sat up and began to speak again to the

attending minister and the spectators, begging them

"heartily to pray for him." Then this intrepid charac-

ter climbed back, unassisted, into the cart. The rope

held the second time.[66]

---

65. _Maryland Gazette_, May 10, 1753; _Pennsylvania
Gazette_, May 17, 1753.

66. _Virginia Gazette_, November 24, 1738. Carts
seemed to have been generally used for the execution of

Declared dead, the body was usually taken down and placed into a coffin, to be claimed by friends and relatives. In the case of Dittond, as reported in the Virginia Gazette, the body was "to be anatomized by the Surgeons." And although Lowe Jackson's crime of counterfeiting was considered treason (which called for his body to be quartered after hanging), his body was placed in a coffin bearing the inscription, "Mercy! triumph over Justice." His friends were allowed to claim the corpse and inter it in his native Nansemond County.[67]

Hangings were by no means limited to the male sex. Women convicted for felony also departed this life from beneath the same gallows as their male counterparts. Nor was there a color line, for Caesar Valentine, a free Negro, was executed upon the local gallows in 1759. Sometimes the spectators who flocked to witness these

---

criminals in the eighteenth century. In the Virginia Gazette (Purdie & Dixon) of August 15, 1766, a hanging in Liverpool, England, is described in which the condemned man was swung off in this fashion. In 1746 the people of Norfolk, Virginia, celebrated the defeat of the Scots at Culloden by hanging an effigy of the Pretender from a cart. (Ibid., July 31, 1746.)

67. Virginia Gazette, November 24, 1738; Pennsylvania Gazette, May 17, 1753; Maryland Gazette, May 10, 1753.

macabre spectacles were well rewarded for their time and effort; upon occasion as many as three, four or even five criminals were executed in a single day. The high mark was reached on November 23, 1739 when seven "Malefactors," including one woman, were "turn'd off."[68]

Death did not always close the book on a crime, for the body was not necessarily allowed to rest in peace. In 1710 Salvadore, an Indian, and Scipio, a Negro slave, were found guilty by the General Court. The Council ordered that they be taken to Gloucester and New Kent Counties for execution. After they had been hanged in the usual manner they were to be decapitated, and then quartered, the heads and quarters to be distributed and displayed "in the most publick place" in various

---

68. _Virginia Gazette_, November 26, 1736, May 23, 1755, November 30, 1759. Originally nine persons had been sentenced to die on this day, but two had been pardoned by the governor. Intercessions had been made on behalf of the others, but their crimes were either unpardonable, or they were old offenders. William Parks took this occasion to comment in his _Virginia Gazette_, on "his Honour's Clemency having been often abus'd by hardened Wretches who had receiv'd the Benefit of his great Lenity, and instead of making a good Use of it, had return'd to, and repeated their wicked courses, it is no wonder his Honour has ordered Justice to be executed on these unhappy deluded Wretches, as Examples to others; tho' so much against his merciful Disposition."

counties throughout the colony as a graphic deterrent to all others who might be inclined to commit similar acts of treason.[69]

A like fate involved one group of pirates. Because these "profligate Wretches...[had] behaved w'th the greatest impudence at the Bar" and were so bold as to have "vented their imprications on their Judges and all concerned in their prosecution, and vow'd if they were at liberty they would spare none alive that should fall into their hands," Governor Spotswood felt that an unusually severe punishment was justified. Therefore, "for the greater Terrour," two of the group were condemned to be hanged in chains on Tindall's Point on the York River, while the other two were to suffer a similar fate at Urbanna on the Rappahannock.[70]

---

69. Exec. Jour. Council Col. Va., III, 242-243. This is only one of two cases where slaves were tried in the General Court. Under ordinary circumstances slaves who had committed a felony were tried under a commission of oyer and terminer issued by the governor. The other case was that of Mary Aggie, a slave belonging to Anne Sullivan of Williamsburg. (See BURGLARY in Chapter IV.)

70. Spotswood to the Board of Trade, May 20, 1720, Brock, Spotswood Letters, II, 337; Exec. Jour. Council Col. Va., III, 521-522.

There were often other ramifications after death. The costs of the prosecution that had brought about his death had to be paid by the condemned man inasmuch as they were levied against his estate. If he was possessed of no property, the costs were assumed by the public.[71] But these were the last assessments against the deceased. Henceforth, he became but a name in the court records, an inscription on a tombstone, or a fleeting memory in the minds of men.

Because of the severity of colonial laws--nearly every felony carried the death penalty--a spot newspaper check was run in an effort to establish a pattern of Virginia justice. In forty-seven court sessions selected at random between 1737 and 1772, a total of 336 persons accused of felonies were brought to trial. Over one-half this number were either acquitted or allowed benefit of clergy. Five received the pardon of the governor in court, while twenty-nine were sentenced to imprisonment or some other punishment short of death. A little over one-third, or 125, received the death penalty, but

---

71. Hening, Statutes, II, 240; Webb, Justice of Peace, pp. 112-113; Starke, Justice of Peace, p. 120.

it seems likely that at least one-fourth of these received a pardon from the governor.[72]

  Crime seldom paid in colonial Virginia, although justice in the highest court was sometimes administered in an amateurish fashion. Yet, on the other
hand, it was tempered with.mercy. And perhaps it was
after contrasting the incidence of crime in England with
that of his own colony that Governor Spotswood was led
to comment in 1720:

> [I] declare sincerely to Yo'r Lord'p
> that I have observed here less swearing and
> Prophaneness, less Drunkeness and Debauch-
> ery, less uncharitable feuds and animositys,
> and less Knaverys and Villanys than in any
> part of the world where my Lot has been, and
> whether the natural Cause of this blessing be
> the people's living under less worldly Temp-
> tations, or being more obedient to their
> Spiritual Pastours, or that they are more
> dexterous in concealing from me their Vices,
> I will not pretend to decide, but resolved
> I am, whether this be the real or my imagin-
> ary State of Virginia, that such a one shall

---

72. These figures were taken from the files of the
Virginia Gazette, the Maryland Gazette, July 26, 1749,
and the Pennsylvania Journal and Weekly Advertiser,
July 26, 1750. The breakdown of the 336 cases were:
deaths, 125; acquitted, 96; burnt in the hand, 81;
pardoned in court, 5; imprisonment, 5; other punishments 24.

be sincerely encouraged here so long as
her Majesty shall think me worthy of serving in this Station....[73]

In contrast with the rather liberal protection

of the rights of the individual in modern courts, the

judicial system of colonial Virginia seems, at best,

crude. Yet it was these practices that provided the

foundations for modern jurisprudence. And whatever the

criticisms, it was justice in their time.

---

73. Spotswood to the Bishop of London, October 24,1710,
Brock,Spotswood Letters, I, 27-28.

Chapter IV

CRIMINAL CASES IN THE GENERAL COURT

Colonial punishments, when contrasted with
those of modern jurisprudence seem, at a casual glance,
to be unduly severe. Yet in the administration of their
criminal statutes the colonials seem to have tempered
their judgments with more mercy than did English courts.
After the Parliament provided for the transportation of
certain convicts to the colonies in 1727 (and the greatest number were sent to Virginia and Maryland) the crime
rate rose, so much so that the attorney-general of Virginia successfully petitioned for an increase in salary
because of the increased demands upon his office. Still,
the increase in crime might also be credited to the colony's expanding population with a greater number of Virginians who were inclined to do evil. Whether the convicts were responsible for the increase in crime or not
seems an academic question; what is more important the
Virginians thought they were. The Virginia Gazette of

September 16, 1737 pointed an accusing finger when it
noted,"There are now in the Publick Prison, no less than
10 Criminals; most of them Convicts, who, poor unhappy
Wretches, cannot leave off their old Trade, tho' they
have had fair Warning, and some of them narrowly escap'd
the Gallows before." And fourteen years later there was
a cynical reflection when the same paper observed:

> When we see our Papers fill'd continually
> with Accounts of the most audacious Rob-
> beries, the most cruel Murders, and in-
> finite other Villanies perpetrated by Con-
> victs transported from Europe, what melan-
> choly, what terrible Reflections must it
> occasion! What will become of our Posterity?
> These are some of thy Favours, Britain! Thou
> are called our Mother Country; but what good
> Mother ever sent Thieves and Villains to
> accompany her Children; to corrupt some with
> their infectious Vices and murder the rest?
> What Father ever endeavour'd to spread the
> Plague in his Family! We do not ask Fish,
> but thou gavest us Serpents, and more than
> Serpents! In what can Britain show a more
> Sovereign contempt for us than by emptying
> their Jails into our Settlements; unless
> they would likewise empty their Jakes on
> our tables?[1]

In the following alphabetical discussion of
crime in eighteenth-century Virginia, there are listed
punishments for felonies that under a modern legal system

---

1. Virginia Gazette, September 16, 1737, May 24,
1751.

would seem inhumane. Yet it should be remembered that the environment was hardly compatible with modern conditions and in a colonial society, isolated from the mother country, harsh punishments were considered deterrents and those concerned cared little for the rehabilitation of persons of criminal intent. The law had not yet outgrown its Mosaic inclinations.

Though there were crimes other than those on the following list that fell within the jurisdiction of the General Court, there is such little evidence that trials concerning them ever came before the higher court, the discussion has either been abbreviated or eliminated entirely.

ARSON

Possibly the most dreaded sound (other than a savage war whoop) in the eighteenth century was the clamor of the fire bell in the night.

Arson of dwelling houses, because of the likelihood of personal danger to the inhabitants therein, was considered a particularly odious crime under English common law. This feeling carried over into Virginia. In

1730, the Assembly passed into statute a bill providing that any person convicted of "maliciously, unlawfully, and willingly" engaging in arson would be adjudged a felon without benefit of clergy.[2]

Arson sometimes rested on an economic foundation. The price of tobacco was the economic barometer of colonial Virginia. When prices declined, there were those who attempted to control the demand by destroying the supply. In 1684, the plant-cutting episodes led to the passage of a law stating that any group of eight or more persons, willfully applying the torch to any building in which tobacco was stored, could "be deemed, declared and adjudged to be traytors, and suffer paines of death, and alsoe loose and forfeite as in cases of high treason." In 1712, after the counties had been empowered to construct public warehouses and fix the rates of storage, there were a number of veiled threats that these structures would be burned. Perhaps it was such threats that prompted the law of 1714 "to prevent the malitious burning or Destroying the Public Store houses

---

2. William Waller Hening, ed., The Statutes at Large: Being a Collection of all the Laws of Virginia from the First Session of the Legislature, in the Year 1619 (New York, 1810-1823), IV, 271-272.

of Tobacco Agents." Under this statute the burning of warehouses was termed a felony, yet it did not take away benefit of clergy. The very next year "the peoples' inclinations...[were] so great against the Tobacco law" that they burned a warehouse in Essex County.[3]

Despite the possibility of felony charges facing a warehouse-burner, these storage sheds continued to go up in flames at almost regular intervals. But it should be noted that the torch was not always applied with an idea of stabilizing tobacco prices. In some instances, the burning of a warehouse concealed a robbery, and it was not unknown that the keeper of a public warehouse commit arson to conceal evidence of his own maladministration.[4]

---

3. Ibid., III, 11, IV, 32-36; H. R. McIlwaine, ed., Journals of the House of Burgesses in Virginia 1712-1714, (Richmond, 1906-1915), pp. xxvii, 116 [hereafter cited as JHB plus date]; Leo Tarent to -----, April 15, 1715, William P. Palmer and others, eds., Calendar of Virginia State Papers and Other Manuscripts, 1652-1781 (Richmond, 1875), I, 181. This law of 1714 is not included in Hening. Only the title, and the order that it be enjoined, appear in the Journals.

4. R. T. Barton, ed., Virginia Colonial Decisions: The Reports by Sir John Randolph and by Edward Barradall of Decisions of the General Court of Virginia, 1728-1741 (Boston, 1909), I, R1, R7, R70-R72.

It was perhaps because of the ineffectual application of the law of 1714 that the statute against burning warehouses was revised in 1730. In his address to the Assembly that year, Governor Gooch declared:

> It will also be worthy of your Consideration to inflict adequate punishments on such offenders as are guilty of the Felonious burning of Tobacco houses, and on robbers of stores and Ware-houses, practices now become very frequent and I am afraid too much encouraged by the allowing of the benefit of Clergy to such Criminals; especially since so many Imported Convicts are come among us who make light of the punishment of the Law in that case inflicts.[5]

The Assembly agreed, and the law passed that session provided the death penalty, without benefit of clergy, for any person, or accessory, burning a tobacco-house, any building containing grain, "or any other houses whatsoever."[6]

Even with this severe penalty, the deterrent was not realized. Within two years after the passage of this statute, warehouses in Northumberland, Lancaster and King George Counties were set aflame "by Some malicious & evil dispos'd persons as yet unknown...." The guilty

---

5. JHB 1727-1734, p. 58.

6. Hening, Statutes, IV, 271.

persons remained at large despite the reward of £100

offered by the governor. This rash of arson led Gooch,

with the advice of the Council, to suggest that special

guards be employed for the warehouses.[7]

Slaves sometimes set fire to tobacco houses

as a method of gaining revenge upon their masters. In

1730, after Justice of the Peace William Harrison had

pronounced sentence upon several Negroes for unlawful

assembly, they retaliated by firing his private tobacco

house.[8]

Almost any fire that occurred in the eighteenth

century was suspected as the work of an arsonist. In

1705 the fire at the College of William and Mary was

thoroughly investigated with a view toward establishing

that premise. And when the Capitol burned in 1747 many

---

7. Proclamation, March 17, 1731, PRO CO5/1323; H. R.
McIlwaine and Wilmer L. Hall, eds., Executive Journals of
the Council of Colonial Virginia (Richmond, 1925-1945),
IV, 259-260, 281, 465-467, 469; JHB 1727-1740, pp. 154,
156-157, 158-159; H. R. McIlwaine, ed., Legislative Journals of the Council of Colonial Virginia (Richmond, 1918-1919),
II, 812; Virginia Gazette, March 17, 1738.

8. JHB 1727-1740, p. 63; JHB 1752-1758, p. 239.

suspected that "it was designedly, wickedly and mali-

ciously contrived & perpetrated...." In a like manner,

when the county courthouse of Southampton burned in 1767,

it was felt that it was the work of an incendiary, and

a reward offered for his apprehension.[9]

Gaols were among those public buildings sub-

ject to the torch of the arsonist. In 1751 Nicholas

Derin, of Amelia, was sentenced to death "for burning

the Prison." Only the vigilance of the public watchman

prevented the public gaol in Williamsburg from suffering

a like fate in 1772. A "Negro Fellow" confined in the

gaol made an ingenious escape by burning a hole in the

floor of his cell, and had the flames not been discovered,

the entire building might well have been consumed.[10]

Even churches were not so sacrosanct that they

escaped the arsonist. In 1732 a reward of £100 was of-

fered for information leading to the conviction of "some

---

9. Exec. Jour. Council Col. Va., V, 488-489; JHB
1720-1712, pp. 139-140; Virginia Gazette (Purdie &
Dixon), June 25, 1767.

10. Virginia Gazette, October 17, 1751, November 19, 1772.

wickid and Evil Disposed Persons" who burned St. Mark's
Church in Spotsylvania County.[11]

Robbery was sometimes the motive for arson.
Stores were burned after being burglarized, as were other
buildings, to hide the evidence of the original crime.
In 1768, when the post office operated by Purdie and
Dixon was robbed, an attempt was made to fire the build-
ing by throwing a shovel of hot coals on a bed.[12]

The burning of dwelling houses remained the
greatest, and an almost continuing fear, in the minds
of the people. As early as 1705, anyone who allowed
brush fires to get from under control to such an extent
that the property of others was damaged, was liable to
a fine and could be assessed double the damage caused
by the flames.[13]

---

11. Exec. Jour. Council Col. Va., IV, 468-469;
Legis. Jour. Council Col. Va., II, 806; JHB 1727-1740,
pp. 151-152, 155.

12. Virginia Gazette (Purdie & Dixon), January 8,
1768, June 1, 1769; JHB 1742-1749, p. 165; JHB 1727-1740,
p. 230.

13. JHB 1702-1712, p. 105. A slave or servant
allowing a fire to get from under his control was subject to corporal punishment.

Premeditated arson was something else again. And the arsonists were seldom apprehended; extant copies of the Virginia Gazette list only one occasion that an arsonist was convicted in the General Court. This was the only conviction out of a regular wave of house burnings between 1768 and 1771. Some of these arson cases were serious enough to prompt the governor to issue proclamations offering rewards for the apprehension of the guilty parties.[14]

Slaves who engaged in the not so gentle art of arson seemed less adept than their white counterparts. They were frequently caught, tried by the county courts of oyer and terminer, convicted and executed. One of these slaves, who burned the "manor house" of Thomas Emerson of Caroline County in 1739, served as an example to others so inclined; after he was hanged, the court ordered his head cut off and set up upon a pole in some public place.[15]

---

14. Virginia Gazette (Purdie & Dixon), February 23, 1769, October 3, 1771; (Rind), September 22, 1768, May 11, 1769.

15. York County Records, Wills, Deeds and Orders, 1728-1732, p.489, and 1768-1770, pp. 419-420, Virginia State Library, Richmond, Virginia; T. C. Campbell, A History of Caroline County, Virginia (Richmond, 1956), p.337.

The winter of 1728-1729 was one in which there was "a great deal of mischief done by Fire...." Robert "King" Carter's "fine House," Corotoman, burned "by what accident they can't tell," with the loss of all his furniture and a wine cellar valued at £500. But the fire that attracted the greatest interest was that which destroyed Mount Pleasant, the home of Thomas Lee in Westmoreland County. Wednesday night, January 29, 1728, was cold, and the fire was already beyond control when it was first discovered. Lee had just enough time to push his pregnant wife, three small children and eight servants--all of them in their night clothes--out of the window before the roof collapsed. A young white girl of twelve years of age perished in the flames. All evidence implied a clear case of arson; a search of the ashes revealed no trace of the large amount of money or silver plate that had been in the house. It was suggested that the fire had been set by the crew of a convict ship in a spirit of revenge. Previously Lee had issued a warrant to the mate of the ship, allowing him to punish several of the crew. Governor Gooch immediately offered £50 for the apprehension of the guilty person or persons, but it was generally felt that they had escaped to another colony. With a bounty granted by the Crown, Lee was able to construct another dwelling, Stratford Hall. Strangely enough, less than a month later, Lee's brother Philip saw every building on his plantation go up in flames, and his "whole family frost-niped before they could gett to shelter."[16]

Arson, although it was greatly feared and often suspected, was seldom proved and punished. And, when fitted into the general pattern of crime in colonial Virginia, it occurred infrequently.

BASTARDY

The punishment of those women who bore illegitimate children did not fall within the province of the General Court--that was for the county courts to decide. It was only when the mothers of such offspring murdered their bastards "to avoid the shame," that the

---

16. Anne Staunton to Thomas Gooch, February 25, 1729, Gooch typescript, Colonial Williamsburg, Inc.; Maryland Gazette, February 4, 1729, March 4, 1729; Gooch to Lords of Trade, January 9, 1730, PRO CO5/1322, Virginia Colonial Records Project microfilm, Colonial Williamsburg, Inc.; Exec. Jour. Council Col. Va., IV, 196.

case fell within the jurisdiction of the higher court.

Because of the circumstances surrounding the death of bastard children, this was one of the few capital crimes in which the burden of proof rested with the defendant. It was the responsibility of the mother to prove, through the testimony of at least one witness, that the child had been born dead, and there had been no criminal intent in her failure to notify the proper authorities of its death.[17]

Although a rather large number of women received the death penalty for concealing the death of their illegitimate children, there were likewise numerous occasions in which the accused woman was acquitted by the jury. There seems to have been a tendency on the part of the Governor and Council to look with some compassion upon unwed females accused of murdering their children. In one case, Ann Tandy of Bruton Parish was presented by the York County Court and charged as an accessory in the death of her infant son. Her indictment in the General Court, however, was changed to

---

17. Hening, Statutes, III, 516-517.

"Concealing ye Death of her Bastard Child," and though
convicted, she later received a pardon from "His Excel-
lency in Council."[18]

A few years later a jurisdictional controversy
arose out of a case in which an unnamed woman was tried
for this felony. It was moved in court, perhaps by her
counsel, that the act of Parliament providing the death
penalty for this crime did not apply to the colonies.
The motion was based on a technicality; since the act
had been passed in 1624, after the settlement of Virginia,
and whereas Virginia had not been specifically named in
this statute, it was argued that its provisions did not
extend to the colony. The court requested "the concur-
rent opinion of the ablest lawyers here," who, in turn,
agreed that the act was not applicable to Virginia. The
defendant was acquitted. But "lest the judgment should
give encouragement to such wicked practices," the Assembly hastily passed "An Act to prevent the destroying and
murdering Bastard Children," couched "in the very terms

---

18. Virginia Gazette, May 6, 1737, June 16, 1738,
May 4, 1739, June 13, 1751, (Purdie & Dixon) April 18,
1771; Exec. Jour. Council Col. Va., II, 154-155, 236-
237; York County Records, Deeds, Orders, Wills, 1698-
1702, p. 518.

of the Act of Parliament with some small variations adapt-
ing it to the circumstances of this country." Such restrictions were necessary; any female indentured servant
who bore an illegitimate child became liable for an additional year of servitude. To circumvent this extra service a woman would quite often destroy her child or conceal the birth of a still-born infant.[19]

Within three years of this controversy, the
Governor and Council became involved in still another
interpretation of the law. Upon this occasion, the point
of argument was whether the governor had the authority to
pardon mothers convicted of murdering their bastard children, or whether an appeal to the crown was necessary.
This question arose out of the case of Jane Ham of Prince
William County, convicted in the April, 1713, session
of the General Court for concealing the death of her
illegitimate child. During the course of the trial, the
evidence indicated that Jane had done no violence to her
baby, and that she had failed to report its death more

---

19. Spotswood to the Lords of Trade, March 6, 1711,
PRO CO6/1363, Va. Col. Rec. microfilm; R. A. Brock, ed.,
The Official Letters of Alexander Spotswood, Lieutenant-
Governor of the Colony of Virginia, 1710-1722 (Richmond,
1932-1935), I, 57-58; Hening, Statutes, III, 456, 516-517.

through ignorance than anything else. Yet, it was ob-

vious that she was guilty. After her conviction, Gov-

ernor Spotswood protested that he could not grant a par-

don to a person convicted of willful murder. The Council

suggested that he reprieve the condemned woman and for-

ward an appeal to the queen.[20]

Spotswood dispatched a letter to Lord Dartmouth,

representing the facts of the case and requesting that

Jane Ham be pardoned by her majesty, the queen. There

was no answer. He wrote again, followed by still an-

other dispatch. Jane Ham had spent a total of eighteen

months in prison when the governor wrote his fourth and

last letter in her behalf. He carefully explained that

although the statute covering the concealment of the

death of bastard children should have been read in all

churches as required by law, he had discovered that it

had not been so published in Jane's parish church. Her

only crime as shown by the evidence, he argued, was not

in murdering her child, but merely concealing its death.

Ignorance and fear that she would be required to serve

20. Exec. Jour. Council Col. Va., III, 344, 346.

her master an extra year were her only crimes.[21]

Still there was no answer from London. In the meantime, Queen Anne died, and the Council of Virginia seemingly felt that with a new monarch on the throne, any additional petitions would be lost in the shuffle. Their advice to the governor was that "tho' the punishment for concealing the death of a Bastard Child is by Law declared to be the same as that of wilful murder, the crime is very different & especially since upon her tryal it did not appear that she had any ways occasioned the death of her Child," and they suggested that the governor pardon her. He did.[22]

Concealment of the death of an infant born in wedlock also fell under the same statute applicable to the death of illegitimate children. One such case involved Sarah Williamson, a married Indian woman who was tried before the General Court in 1728. Governor

---

21. Spotswood to Dartmouth, June 30, 1713, PRO CO5/1337, Va. Col. Rec. microfilm; Spotswood to Dartmouth, May 13, 1713, and to Lord Bolingbroke, n.d., Brock, Spotswood Letters, II, 19, 74.

22. Exec. Jour. Council Col. Va., III, 391-392.

William Gooch was particularly impressed with "her Christian behaviour during the time of her trial and imprisonment, her resignation under her sentence, her willingness to
die, and at the same time her constancy in denying the
fact." He convinced himself that she was not guilty.
Her only crime, he felt, was her ignorance in burying
the child without informing the proper authorities. His
eloquent plea to the crown on behalf of this poor Indian
woman was successful, although two years were to pass before the pardon was finally returned from England.[23]

Because of the large number of indentured and
convict servants in colonial Virginia, and because the
morals of these servants did not always follow delicate
lines, bastardy was fairly common in the seventeenth century when indentured servants were more numerous than
slaves. The problem was primarily economic, and county
courts punished the parents for their indiscretions and
arranged for the support of the child. It was only after
the murder of the child, or its burial without proper
notification that the case reached the General Court.

---

23. Gooch to "Your Grace," July 9, 1728, PRO CO5/
1337, Va. Col. Rec. microfilm; Exec. Jour. Council Col.
Va., IV, 213.

BLASPHEMY

This crime was committed when:

> any person or persons brought up in the chris-
> tian religion shall be writeing, printing,
> teaching or advisedly speakeing, deny the
> being of a God or the holy Trinity or shall
> assert or maintaine there are more Gods than
> one or shall deny the christian religion to
> be true, or the holy scriptures of Old and
> New Testament to be of divine authority....[24]

After his first conviction, a blasphemer was

denied the right to hold office, ecclesiastical, civil,

or military. A second conviction stripped him of all

citizenship rights. If, however, he recanted his blas-

phemous statements within six months of his conviction,

and in the same court in which he was found guilty, all

disabilities were removed.[25]

From the available court records, it seems

that the statute against blasphemy was seldom exercised

in the General Court during the eighteenth century.

---

24. Hening, Statutes, III, 168. This was almost
word for word a duplicate of a similar law passed by the
English Parliament in 1698. (Sir James Fitzjames Stephen,
A History of the Criminal Law of England [London, 1883],
II, 468.)

25. Hening, Statutes, III 169.

Indeed, in 1730 the preamble for an act "for the effectual suppression of Vice," stated that the former law "hath not been duly put into execution, according to the intent and design thereof; whereby divers wicked and dissolute persons have been encouraged to commit the crimes therein mentioned...."[26]

The only semblance of a trial for blasphemy occurred in 1754, when one William Sherring was sentenced to die for "sacrilege," which certainly falls within the limits of the law. Although the law specified trials in the General Court for blasphemous offences, most ecclesiastical causes of a serious nature seem to have been examined by the Governor in Council. Many charges involving religion were not so much concerned with blasphemous utterances as with complaints made by vestries of the immoralities of their ministers. Two near-blasphemous charges were recorded in 1734 and 1752. The first was made against the Reverend Mr. Staige of York County for refusing to christen bastard children and opposing the singing of the "new version of Psalmes." Eighteen years later the Reverend Alexander Craighead

---

26. Ibid., IV, 244.

of Augusta was brought before the Governor and Council
for preaching and publishing "pernicious Doctrines." No
real punishment was handed down in either case, with
Mr. Staige promising to behave himself in the future,
and Mr. Craighead "taking the oaths to Government openly
in the General Court."[27]

A general charge against the blasphemous spirit
of the times was made by the Council in an address to
Governor Gooch in 1747. It seems to have been directed
against the Reverend George Whitefield, who had preached
in Virginia just two years earlier and whose doctrines
at that time had been denounced in the Virginia Gazette.
This was shortly after the burning of the Capitol, which
the Council blamed on past sins and,

> a Spirit of Enthusiasm introduced among the
> the People by Itinerant Preachers; a Spirit,
> more dangerous to the common Welfare, than

---

27. Virginia Gazette, November 7, 1754; "Virginia
Council Journals," May 11, 1742, Virginia Magazine of
History and Biography, XV (April, 1908), 377; Exec. Jour.
Council Col. Va., IV, 89-90, 384, 413, V, 399, 407-408;
Landon C. Bell, ed., Charles Parish, York County, Virginia History and Registers, Birth, 1648-1739, Deaths
1665-1787 (Richmond, 1932), p. 28. In 1775, Edward Brown
of Charles City County was tried for sacrilege, but acquitted. (Virginia Gazette [Purdie], October 27, 1775.)

the furious Element, which laid the Royal
Edifice in Ashes; a Spirit, productive not
only of Confusion, but of Blasphemy, Profaneness, and the most wickid & destructive
Practices....[28]

On the whole, blasphemy seems to have been of much greater concern in the seventeenth century than the eighteenth, perhaps a reflection of the growing sophistication among the Virginians. In those rare instances when it did occur, the case was usually taken care of in the county courts, although there was a growing concern among the Anglicans who blamed dissenting sects for spreading blasphemous doctrines among the people. It was probably because of the existence of fairly stringent legal restrictions that these dissenters did not openly "continue their impious and abominable practices and avow their horrid and Atheisticall principles greatly tending to the dishonour of Almighty God."[29]

---

28. Legis. Jour. Council Col. Va., II, 995-996;
Virginia Gazette, October 10 and 31, 1745.

29. Hening, Statutes, III, 168.

BIGAMY

Bigamy was a felony that was never a great problem for colonial Virginians. The only statute concerned with multiple marriage listed in the laws was dated 1658, and it merely stated that the same laws against bigamy then prevalent in England would "be put in execution in this countrie."[30]

Although bigamy was classed as a felony, it was still not considered too horrendous a crime, for it was one of those misadventures for which benefit of clergy was allowed. There were also several exceptions to the general conception of bigamy under which a man might remarry, although his first wife be still living. Restrictions upon taking a second mate did not apply to a person whose husband or wife had been "beyond the Seas" for a period of seven years or longer, and it was not known whether the former husband or wife was still living. Marriages dissolved by ecclesiastical courts were considered to be null and void, and the participants were absolved of any legal restrictions in remarrying.

---

30. *Ibid.*, I, 434.

In a like manner, in a marriage when either or both participants were below the age of consent (fourteen years
for a man; twelve for a maid), the contract could be
terminated by agreement at any time before the age of
consent was reached, leaving both parties free to remarry without hazard.[31]

On the whole, colonial Virginians seemed to
have felt that one wife was enough at any one time. And
then, too, there never seemed enough women to go around.
The eighteenth-century records contain reference to only
two men, and no women, standing trial in the General
Court for bigamy. In each instance the defendants, John
Burgard of Caroline County and Stephen Hutchins of Norfolk, were acquitted.[32]

---

31. George Webb, The Office and Authority of a Justice of Peace....(Williamsburg, 1736), pp. 60-61; Richard
Starke, The Office and Authority of a Justice of Peace,
Explained and Digested, Under Proper Titles (Williamsburg,
1774), pp. 276-277.

32. Virginia Gazette (Rind), April 18, 1755,
April 22, 1773.

BURGLARY

William Byrd II of Westover, a judge in the
General Court, was on the periphery of perjury when he
wrote in 1726:

> we sit securely under our Vines and Fig Trees
> without any Danger to our Property. We have
> neither publick Robbers or private, which Your
> Ldsp will think very strange, when we have of-
> ten needy Governors, and pilfering Convicts
> sent amongst us....Then we have no such Trades
> carried on amongst us, as that of Horsebreakers
> [housebreakers?] Highwaymen, or Beggars. We
> can rest securely in our Beds with all our
> Doors and Windows open, and yet find every
> thing exactly in place the next Morning. We
> can travel all over the Country by Night and
> by Day, unguarded and unarmed, and never meet
> with any Person so rude as to bid us Stand.[33]

But Byrd was writing of his native Virginia to a London

acquaintance, and his letter may be forgiven for its en-

thusiastic tone and proud puffings. Indeed, burglary and

robbery in all its forms plagued the colony throughout

the colonial era.

The crime of taking something from another with-

out consent fell under many classifications; burglary,

robbery, larceny, picking pockets, hog-stealing,

---

33. William Byrd to Charles, Earl of Orrery, July 5,
1726, Virginia Magazine of History and Biography, XXXII
(January, 1924), 27.

horse-stealing, and Negro-stealing. Each of these sub-
divisions, for the sake of convenience, will be dis-
cussed under separate subheadings.

Burglary was defined as the "breaking and entering of a Mansion-house, in the Night Time, with an
Intent to kill, or steal, though none be killed, nor any
Thing stolen." Churches and all public buildings were
considered "Mansion-houses" under the law, as were all
outbuildings contiguous to a dwelling. Originally, it
was required that a theft be valued at five shillings
or more before it became capital, but in 1730 this min-
imum was raised to twenty shillings, lawful money. The
punishment for burglary was death by hanging and the
crime was not clergyable. Accessories before the fact
were likewise denied clergy while accessories after the
fact were granted this boon.[34]

The crime of burglary required the involve-
ment of several specifics before it could be classified
as such. In the first place, there had to be an actual

---

    34. Webb, <u>Justice of Peace</u>, p. 63; Hening, <u>Statutes</u>,
IV, 272.

breaking in. A thief entering the open doors or windows of a house could not be accused of breaking and entering. Yet, on the other hand, if he entered with a key, or came down a chimney, in either case with the aid of an accomplice, it was considered breaking and entering as though he smashed a door or broke a window. He was also considered guilty of burglary if he drew goods through a window with his hands or by aid of a hook, or even if he had acted as a look-out for those who actually committed the crime.[35]

There was a valid reason for limiting the crime of burglary to a time of darkness, the difference between night and day defined as; "whereby a Man's Countenance may be discerned, it is called Day; and when Darkness comes, and Day Light is passed, so by the Light of Day you cannot discern the Countenance of a Man, then it is called Night." In 1774 Richard Starke explained the reasoning behind the limitation of a burglary to night:

> this doth aggravate the Offence, since the
> Night is the Time wherein Man is at Rest,

---

35. Webb, Justice of Peace, p. 63.

and wherein Beasts run about seeking their
Prey. Hence, in ancient Records, the Twi-
light was signified when it was said <u>inter</u>
<u>canem</u> <u>et</u> <u>lupum</u> (between the Dog and the
Wolf) for when the Night begins, the Dog
sleeps, and the Wolf seeketh his Prey.[36]

In burglary trials, it was the responsibility
of the prosecution to prove the intent of the accused.
Unless it could be established that the person on trial
held intentions to kill or steal, there could be no felony. There was an element of double jeopardy here, for
a person acquitted of burglary could still be indicted
for larceny. Intent sometimes had to be proved by the
person robbed. If a house had been unoccupied at the
time of the deed, the absent resident had to prove his
intentions of returning to that habitation before the
alleged thief could be charged with burglary.[37]

Burglars usually concentrated their attentions
upon dwelling houses and stores. Sometimes there was
violence, as in the case of a reputed miser in Nansemond
County. Four desperadoes, two of them disguised, broke

---

36. Starke, <u>Justice of Peace</u>, p. 64.

37. <u>Ibid.</u>, pp. 64-65; Webb, <u>Justice of Peace</u>,
p. 64.

into his home, tied him and his four slaves to their beds, and made off with about £60 in cash.[38]

Norfolk, as other port towns, experienced an almost continuous crime wave. This was particularly true in the 1760's. In the early years of the decade, the officials of Norfolk petitioned the House of Burgesses for legislation allowing the city to assess additional taxes to raise the necessary funds to employ a night watch and erect street lamps. These precautions did little to alleviate the situation, and there were increasing burglaries similar to that reported by John Greenhow, whose Norfolk warehouse was robbed of twenty-five greatcoats. In 1771 this flush of criminal activity was curbed somewhat when it was discovered that a gang of thieves had been operating in the area. A number of this group were apprehended and incarcerated. The house of one of their members proved to be a veritable storehouse of stolen property. Clothing and dry goods were concealed beneath the floor, while the risers leading to the upper floor had been converted into drawers which could be pulled out and filled with loot. The attic of

---

38. Virginia Gazette, April 29, 1737.

the house "resembled a warehouse." Perhaps the most ingenious of the Norfolk criminal element was the agile
Thomas Seale, who, while he was in prison, escaped through
the chimney, burglarized the same house he had been indicted for robbing earlier, and then returned to prison
through the chimney in order to cast suspicion from him.[39]

Williamsburg likewise had its habitual criminals, one of the most active bearing the name of Thomas
Arthurnot Grayland. After a number of the stores and
cellars of the city had been entered, Grayland's house
was searched. In a concealed cellar the searchers found
a quantity of bacon, along with the skin and hooves of a
sheep buried beneath the floor. In addition to tools
which might be used in burglary attempts, Grayland was
found to have in his possession a large number of "false
keys," one master key fitting the locks of all those
places that had been robbed. He was brought before the
next court of oyer and terminer, found guilty and sentenced to hang. Although there is no record of it, he

39. JHB 1761-1765, p. 183; Hening, Statutes, VII,
654; Virginia Gazette (Purdie & Dixon), September 26, 1766;
Maryland Gazette, January 3, 1771, July 26, 1749; Pennsylvania Gazette, August 5, 1749.

was apparently pardoned and journeyed to Annapolis.

Three months later when a number of cellars and homes in

the Maryland capital were looted without a single lock

broken, William Rind speculated in the Virginia Gazette

that Grayland was once again "pursuing his old occupa-

tion." One example of Grayland's work may have been the

burglarizing of Purdie and Dixon's post office when the

thief attempted to fire the building to conceal his

crime.[40]

There seems to have been little robbery of

government institutions. The nearest thing to a crime

of this nature was the theft of £254.18.9 in quitrent

money placed for safe-keeping in the Williamsburg store

of Archibald Blair in 1722. On the other hand, assuming

that tobacco warehouses were semi-public establishments,

these institutions were frequently broken into and robbed,

especially in the 1760's.[41]

---

40. Virginia Gazette (Purdie & Dixon), January 7,
May 26, June 16, 1768, (Rind) September 22, 1768.

41. Exec. Jour. Council Col. Va., IV, 17; JHB 1758-
1761, pp. 241, 222, 227; JHB 1761-1765, pp. 176, 316-317,
340; JHB 1766-1769, pp. 193, 271, 288-289, 303; JHB
1770-1772, p. 43. In 1691, Edward Banks received an
unique sentence in the York County Court for stealing
tobacco. He was sentenced to receive thirty-nine lashes

Not even the wearers of the cloth, or the churches they served, were inviolate where men of evil intent were concerned. In 1737, three men were hanged for stealing clothing from the home of Reverend Mr. Mortland. In 1748 several felons were apprehended and charged with taking the communion plate from churches throughout the colony; articles usually stolen from churches included communion plate, the cloths covering the altar and communion tables, and even the gowns or surplices of the minister. An unusually enterprising church thief was Robert Alsworthy of Westmoreland County. He filched the purple pulpit cloth of Appomattox Church in Washington Parish, from which he made himself a pair of velvet breeches. But unlike most of those who robbed churches, he was caught wearing the evidence and tried before the General Court.[42]

---

on his bare back, twenty of which were to be inflicted immediately "with some bundles of Tobacco hanging about his neck." The other nineteen were applied at the tobacco house of Joseph Frythe in Bruton Parish, the scene of the robbery. He was then returned to prison until he had paid for the tobacco and the costs of the trial. (York County Records, Deeds, Orders, Wills, 1691-1694, p.90.)

42. Virginia Gazette, May 27, 1737, July 3, 1746, May 15, 1752, December 15, 1768; JHB 1742-1749, p. 303; Charles Arthur Hoppin, "The Pulpit Cloth of Appomattox

Negroes who engaged in burglary were tried in the county courts under a commission of oyer and terminer. Because they were valuable property, and the government reimbursed the owner of a slave hanged for a felony, the punishment for slaves does not always seem so severe as that meted out to their white counterparts. Kate, belonging to Archibald Blair, stole a silk apron and a cambric handkerchief from Elizabeth Russel in 1729. The York County Court sentenced her to receive twenty lashes in Yorktown and on the following day a like number at the public whipping post in Williamsburg. The crime of John Randolph's Ned was considered to be more serious. In November, 1774, he broke into Christiana Campbell's tavern and stole a large amount of clothing from the merchant, Simon Fraser. After evaluating his worth at £80, the court sentenced him to hang.[43]

One case of particular interest involving a slave charged with burglary was that of Mary Aggie, belonging to the Williamsburg innkeeper, Anne Sullivan,

---

Church," William and Mary Quarterly, 1st series, XXVII (July, 1918), 28-33.

43. Virginia Gazette (Purdie & Dixon), June 6, 1766, May 26, 1768; York County Records, Orders, Wills, 1729-1732, part II, p. 592; York County Records, Order Book, 1729-1748, p. 60.

widow of Jean Marot. Mary Aggie broke into the house of
her mistress in 1730 and stole goods to the value of
forty shillings. After the York County Court found her
guilty, a perplexing problem arose. Mary Aggie, when
asked if there was any reason why sentence should not be
passed on her, shrewdly plead benefit of clergy, declaring that she was entitled to it as a Christian. The
question was too difficult to be answered by the county
justices, and their proceedings were turned over to the
General Court for disposition. Governor Gooch decided
that Mary Aggie's claim should be made a test case and
brought her claim before the Council. In their decision
the Council vote was split six and six. Mary Aggie was
then granted a pardon by the governor on condition that
she be transported to the West Indies and there sold
into slavery. The disturbing question of whether slaves
should be granted benefit of clergy was decided two years
later, in 1732, when Negro slaves, by statute, were extended benefit of clergy in all instances as free men
except manslaughter and breaking and entering when goods
worth five shillings sterling or more were taken.[44]

---

44. York County Records, Orders, Wills, 1729-1732,
p. 113; Exec. Jour. Council Col. Va., IV, 243; Hening,

Burglary was a fairly frequent crime in colonial Virginia, but it seemed to reach its peak in the 1760's. Whether or not this was the result of the increasing influx of convicts cannot be accurately determined, but it can be noted that complaints of England's practice of dumping her criminals in the colonies appeared with increasing frequency after 1750.

Robbery

Eighteenth-century legal writers defined robbery as "the felonious and violent taking away from the Person of a Man, or from his House, Goods or Money to any Value, putting him in Fear."[45] Fear, then, was the determining factor in distinguishing robbery from other variations of burglary.

A person who committed robbery and later repented and attempted to return the stolen property had as his only reward a clear conscience; he was still guilty of robbery. All accessories, even those who acted as look-outs and did not participate in the actual crime, were just as guilty as those who were responsible for

---

Statutes, IV 326.

45. Starke, Justice of Peace, p. 310.

taking the goods. Robbery was punishable by death, with the felon excluded from benefit of clergy.[46]

Many robberies occurred on the highway, and the threat was constant enough to make travellers extremely cautious about displaying their wealth in strange places. A large number of these crimes were committed by runaway slaves and servants, and the highwaymen of the day seem to have been characterized by their youthfulness.[47]

Regular organized gangs of robbers quite often resorted to subterfuge to gain entrance to the house or store of their victim. Several of them would gather and knock upon the front door of the building, supposedly upon a legitimate errand. Once the door was opened they would rush in, bind those present and conduct their looting without interference. A gang utilizing this modus operandi were operating in Virginia in 1737.[48]

---

46. Ibid., pp. 310-311.

47. Holderness to the Lords of Trade, March 26, 1752, PRO CO5/1327, Va. Col. Rec. microfilm; Virginia Gazette, June 17, 1737, June 6, 1745, May 24, 1751, March 20, 1752, October 17, 1755, (Purdie & Dixon) May 26, 1768.

48. Virginia Gazette, April 29, September 16, 1737.

In backcountry Virginia and Maryland a gang under the leadership of one Utie Perkins resembled the western outlaws of the next century in their operations. Mounted and armed, they ranged the countryside, bold and strong enough to rob during the daylight hours and "greatly molesting and terrifying the Inhabitants." There is no record of the final disposition of the Perkins gang, although it was noted that several of them were killed while attempting a highway robbery.[49]

Robbery seems to have been the livelihood adopted by many of the runaway servants who dared not return to civilization. Despite the prevalence of robbery, relatively few of the robbers were apprehended.

Larceny

Larceny was still another variant of stealing, defined as the "felonious taking and carrying away" the goods of one person by another. The two gradations of larceny--grand and petit--were determined by the value of the goods stolen.[50]

---

49. Ibid., July 10, 1752; Maryland Gazette, June 5, 1751; JHB 1752-1758, p. 48; Virginia Historical Register and Literary Notebook, III (April, 1850), 75.

50. Webb, Justice of Peace, p. 208; Starke, Justice of Peace, p. 253.

Grand larceny occurred when the value of the stolen goods was evaluated at more than twelve pence. This was a felony, but a first offender was entitled to benefit of clergy. Petit larceny occurred when the value of the goods was less than twelve pence. This was likewise considered a felony, but did not carry the death penalty. The reasoning behind this was that indictments for both grand and petit larceny had to include the word "feloniously" in them; therefore both Webb and Starke argued that petit larceny had to be a felony. The offender, however, did face a forfeiture of his goods and whipping or some other corporal punishment. And petit larceny was one instance in which a man could stand mute and not automatically receive the death penalty. Persons charged with petit larceny were usually tried by the county courts and their punishment was, in general, administered by the whip, sentences ranging from five to thirty-nine lashes.[51]

Grand larceny, being a true felony, was tried in the General Court. A surprisingly large number of

---

51. York County Records, Orders and Wills, 1729-1732, p. 307; York County Records, Wills and Inventories, 1740-1746, p. 398.

people tried for this crime were acquitted. Many instances of grand larceny never came before any court,
primarily because the culprits were never caught; the
most frequent occurrences of this crime were the stealing of boats by runaway slaves and servants to further
their escapes. Negro slaves indicted for grand larceny
were tried in the county courts under a commission of
oyer and terminer, and although they usually received
the death sentence, a pardon was sometimes granted by
the governor upon intercession by their masters. One
of the most unique sentences recorded in the York County
records was that received by Sam, Jack and Cornelius,
Negro slaves accused of grand larceny. Although all
three were found not guilty, it appeared "to the Court
that all the said slaves have misbehaved themselves."
Thus, on what appears to be little more than the prin-
ciple of the thing, two of the slaves received thirty-
nine lashes, while the other was given thirty-five.[52]

Grand larceny was a crime of extensive scope,
and it appears that many of those charged with this

---

52. York County Records, Order Book, 1765-1768,
pp. 23, 44-45.

crime in the public notices had actually committed burglary, but this is impossible to determine without the
court records, and those of the eighteenth-century General Court are but few in number.

Pick-Pockets

Picking pockets fell under the general heading of larceny, and the amount taken determined whether
it was to be classified grand or petit. Again, if the
amount taken was above twelve pence it became grand larceny without benefit of clergy. The crime of picking
pockets was described as "Stealing from the Person, without putting him in Fear, for it is done clandestinely,
and secretly, without his knowledge...."[53]

There were four conditions that had to be
present before picking pockets could be considered a
capital crime; it must have been done clandestinely and
secretly; the thief must have the stolen articles in his
possession when apprehended; it must be done without
putting the person robbed in fear; and the value of the
stolen property must be above twelve pence. If the
amount was less, and the pickpocket was convicted of

---

53. Webb, Justice of Peace, p. 147.

petit larceny, he could be whipped and his goods forfeited.[54]

The county court records contain some mention
of pickpockets, but the crime was seldom listed on the
docket of the General Court. On November 6, 1771, a
"Gentleman" had his pockets picked of £20 while in Williamsburg, but the thief escaped. The only two cases of
picking pockets of a large amount involved two practi-
tioners of the art who were hailed before the high court
in Williamsburg; John Clifton in 1752, and John Derby
(alias Derby Finn) in 1769, both of whom were found
guilty and received the death sentence.[55]

There is little evidence to explain why picking pockets was so little practiced in colonial Virginia.
The severe penalty could have been a deterrent, but more
likely explanations include practical considerations;
pickpockets could work efficiently only in crowds, and
Virginia's rural society offered relatively few oppotun-
ities for the exercise of the art under ideal conditions.

---

54. Ibid., p. 147.

55. Virginia Gazette, December 15, 1752, (Purdie &
Dixon) June 1, 1769, November 7, 1771.

The scarcity of coins and currency and the extensive use of a complicated credit system based on bills of exchange that had to be validated by signatures emptied Virginia pockets of their best pickings.

Hog-Stealing

As early as 1623, Governor Francis Wyatt issued a proclamation "against stealing of beasts and birds of domesticall or tame nature" and announced that those guilty would be punished by "no lesse than death." This seems to have been only a temporary measure, and by 1647 hog stealing was felt to be a crime "seldom or never detected or prosecuted in this collony," and statutes made a person found guilty of killing another's hogs liable to two years servitude as an indentured servant.[56]

In the eighteenth century, a hog thief was tried in the county courts for the first two offences. The first conviction brought a sentence of twenty-five lashes "well laid on" (thirty-nine if the thief was a slave) at the public whipping post of the county in which

---

56. *William and Mary Quarterly*, 2nd series, VII (October, 1927), 252-253; Hening, *Statutes*, I, 350-351. An earlier law of 1642 had made this a felony.

the crime had been committed. A person convicted a second time received his punishment at the county court-house on court day. He was to stand in the pillory with both ears nailed to it. At the end of two hours the ears were "cut loose from the nails." In addition to this disfigurement they were forced to pay the owner of the stolen animals 400 pounds of tobacco for every hog stolen. This decision, however, could be appealed to the General Court. If a person with a particular fond-ness for pork was caught stealing hogs a third time, he was tried before the General Court. A guilty verdict carried the death sentence without benefit of clergy. Because ownership of hogs was indicated by ear notches, any person who carried a hog without ears onto his property could be judged a hog thief unless he could prove it to be his own animal.[57]

One interesting case involving animal stealing involved Henry Downs, a member of the House of Burgesses in 1742. It was reported that Downs (at that time an indentured servant) had been convicted in Maryland in

57. Hening, Statutes, II, 440-441, III, 276-279, VI, 121-124.

1721 of stealing "one Sheep, of a White Colour," for which he had received fifteen lashes and had been pilloried for an hour. The House of Burgesses disabled and expelled Mr. Downs for his indiscretion of twenty-one years earlier.[58]

In general, the people of the colony, excluding slaves, never committed the third offence of hog-stealing. If so, the extant records conceal the true designation of their crimes under the broader listings of "Felony" or "Grand Larceny."

Horse-Stealing

Horses in colonial Virginia were as valuable to their owners as the fabled steeds of the Arabs or the cowboys of western America, and the crime of horse-stealing carried a penalty of death without benefit of clergy.[59]

By 1748, horse-stealing was so frequent that strict controls were placed upon those "divers vagrant people [who] travel through this colony, from the northern provinces, to the southern, pedling, and selling horses, and either buy, or steal, great numbers...." Those who

---

58. JHB 1742-1749, pp. 11, 53.

59. Starke, Justice of Peace, p. 89.

purchased horses they knew to be stolen were subject to the death penalty upon conviction. The Assembly posted a standing reward for the apprehension of horse thieves and granted the families of those killed while endeavoring to apprehend such thieves an indemnity of £50.[60]

The Gazette was filled with advertisements for runaway servants or slaves who stole horses to further their escape. Hanging was mandatory when either slaves or servants were found guilty of horse-stealing. They were not always discriminating in their choice of animals, certainly not leather worker William Quirk, who rode away on his master's "old crop-ear'd, Flea-bitten, white Horse, with a Switch-tail."[61]

Around the middle of the eighteenth century, horse-stealing became "very common, and a growing Evil...," particularly on the frontier. In 1748 horse thieves of the western counties "established themselves into a Confederacy for carrying on that Practice" with the stolen animals usually passed on to accomplices for sale in other colonies. Earlier, Ephraim Biswell of Orange County,

60. Hening, Statutes, VI, 124-131.

61. Virginia Gazette, June 20, 1745.

confessed that he was the member of a gang of ten or more who had managed to steal at least twenty-five horses.[62]

Probably one of the most genteel trials for horse-stealing occurred in York County in 1682. Here the thief was forced to apologize to the plaintiff for stealing his horse. After his apology was accepted, the defendant paid the court costs and the fee of the plaintiff's attorney and was allowed to go his way.[63] Things were not conducted in so casual a manner in the eighteenth century, when many executions were carried through for horse-stealing. There were few pardons. On the other hand, it should be noted that the number of thieves apprehended was small when contrasted with the number of animals stolen.

Negro-Stealing

A Negro slave in colonial Virginia represented a considerable investment, and inasmuch as he was

---

62. Ibid., May 16, 1745; "Moravian Diaries of Travels through Virginia," Virginia Magazine of History and Biography, XII (October, 1904), 151; JHB 1742-1749, p. 274; Arthur P. Scott, Criminal Law in Colonial Virginia (Chicago, 1930), p. 223.

63. York County Records, Deeds, Orders, Wills, 1677-1684, p. 377.

negotiable property and easily transported, the tempta-
tion to steal slaves was strong among the criminally inclined. In fact, Negro, mulatto and Indian slaves were
classified, by a statute of 1705, as real estate. Because there was no law prohibiting the near impossible
crime of stealing real estate, death without benefit of
clergy was prescribed for all those found guilty of
slave-stealing.[64]

Instances of Negro-stealing were frequent in
the eighteenth century, but trials for this felony seldom appeared on the docket of the General Court, suggesting a degree of cleverness among those engaging in the
practice. Stolen slaves were usually taken to another
colony for sale. In the late seventeenth century, there
was some concern expressed about the Indians who were
stealing slaves and selling them in Pennsylvania. Some
years later, Jeremiah Whitney of Virginia, "a tall young
Man, of a fresh Complexion," travelled southward to North
Carolina to do his slave-stealing. Conversely, Virginia
slaves were sometimes "feloniously seduced and conveyed

---

64. Hening, Statutes, III, 333-335, VI, 369.

away....into the Province of North Carolina."[65]

The files of the Virginia Gazette reveal only three instances of persons tried before the General Court for Negro-stealing. Two were acquitted, the third found guilty. The guilty party, however, did not meet his death swinging at the end of a rope; he was pardoned by the governor on condition that he enlist in the crew of H.M.S. Boston, just then sailing for England.[66]

Negro-stealing was one of those crimes that plagued the planters of colonial Virginia throughout the period, but in a community based on a slave economy the theft of such property might well be considered an occupational hazard.

CONSPIRACY

Under English common law, conspiracy held an implication of a combination of two or more persons planning to accuse unjustly or to harm another. Under its

---

65. Exec. Jour. Council Col. Va., I, 262; Virginia Gazette, January 5, 1739, November 21, 1745.

66. Virginia Gazette (Purdie & Dixon), May 7, June 11, 1772, October 21, 1773, April 21, 1774, (Purdie) October 27, 1775.

original meaning, conspiracy was akin to perjury, for
the crime was often outright lying on the witness stand.
Those convicted of conspiracy were liable to a twofold
penalty; they could be required to pay damages or, in
extreme cases, lose their citizenship, forfeit "Lands,
Goods, and Chattels,...and their Bodies imprisoned."[67]

For eighteenth-century Virginians, the fear of
a slave conspiracy lent a dire meaning to the word. This
fear was cogently expressed by William Byrd when he noted,
"Numbers make them insolent, and then foul Means must do
what fair will not...but these base tempers require to
be rid with a tort Rein, or they will be apt to throw
their Rider."[68]

It was in the spring of 1710 that the colony
experienced one of the first serious alarms of this
nature. It happened in Surry County, where a large number of slaves, both Negro and Indian, planned their escape, cutting down all who dared oppose them. The ringleaders were two Negroes, William Edwards' Scipio,

---

67. Webb, Justice of Peace, p. 88; Starke, Justice
of Peace, pp. 100-102.

68. William Byrd to Lord Egmont, July 12, 1736,
American Historical Review, I (January, 1895), 89.

Samuel Thompson's Peter, and the Indian slave, Salvadore, belonging to Joseph Jackman. The plot failed, primarily because Will, a slave owned by Robert Ruffin, reported the planned insurrection.[69]

Peter was apparently successful in his escape, for there is no record of his capture, despite the issuance of a proclamation and the offer of a reward by Edmund Jenings, President of the Council. Conspirators of lesser importance, including those who had known about but had not reported the conspiracy, were tried in the county courts. Their punishments ranged from twenty to thirty-nine lashes at the whipping post. Because of the nature of their crime, Scipio and Salvadore were brought to Williamsburg, indicted for high treason, tried, convicted and sentenced to be hanged, drawn and quartered. Will, the informer, was granted his freedom by the Assembly.[70]

---

69. Cal. Va. St. Papers, I, 129-130; JHB 1702-1712, p. 282.

70. Edmund Jenings to the Board of Trade, April 24, 1710, PRO CO5/1317, Va. Col. Rec. microfilm; Cal. Va. St. Papers, I, 129; Exec. Jour. Council Col. Va., III, 236, 242-243, 246, 573-574, 575; Louis B. Wright and Marion Tinling, eds., The Secret Diary of William Byrd of Westover, 1709-1712 (Richmond, 1941), pp. 167-169; JHB 1702-1712, pp. 270, 294, 298.

In 1723 there was the threat of another slave uprising. Although there was not enough evidence to indict the leaders for high treason, it was ordered that they be transported out of the colony and sold in the West Indies. This intrigue did force the Assembly to take some action against future conspiracies. In his opening address to the House of Burgesses, Governor Drysdale commented on "ye Lameness" of laws against slave conspiracies and then added, "I am persuaded you are too well acquainted with the Cruel dispositions of those Creatures, when they have it in their power to destroy or distress, to lett Slipp this faire opportunity of making more propper Laws against them...."[71]

The result of this suggestion was the passage of "divers good and wholesome regulations for their better government...." This statute stated that when five or more slaves were "consulting, plotting, or conspiring" to "rebel or make insurrection, or shall plot or conspire the murder of any person or persons whatsoever," they were to be judged felons, suffering the death penalty

---

71. Exec. Jour. Council Col. Va., IV, 21, 31; JHB 1712-1716, p. 367; Virginia Historical Register, III (April, 1851), 63.

upon conviction, "and shall be utterly excluded the benefit of clergy." Henceforth slaves, mulattoes, or Indians accused of conspiracy were to be tried in the county courts under a commission of oyer and terminer issued by the governor.[72]

These rigorous restrictions did not completely awe the slaves. In 1730 a rumor spread among the Negroes that an order had been dispatched from England that decreed that all Christian slaves be freed, but this order had been suppressed by the Virginia government. Although the first rumblings of a slave conspiracy were quickly put down "by Imprisonment and severe whippings of the most Suspected," the movement remained active. Some six weeks later, while their masters were at church, about 200 slaves gathered one Sunday and elected officers to command them in a planned revolt. But once again the conspiracy was revealed, and the four principal leaders were tried in the county courts and hanged. Although Governor Gooch observed that "the greater Number, having kind Masters, live much better than our poor labouring

---

72. Drysdale to Lords of Trade and Plantations, PRO CO5/1319, Va. Col. Rec. microfilm; Hening, Statutes, IV, 126-127.

Men in England," he ordered the militia to carry their

arms to church and maintain regular patrols, lest "the

same mutinous Spirit" return. Six years later, these

patrols were still being conducted as a safeguard

against an insurrection of the slaves.[73]

In 1770, an almost spontaneous insurrection

broke out in Hanover County, resulting in a pitched

battle between fifteen white men and forty or fifty

slaves. The fighting died out only after three of the

slaves had been killed, and five wounded.[74]

Slave insurrections remained a constant threat

to the Virginians until 1863, and there were nineteenth-

century conspiracies and insurrections more terrible in

---

73. Gooch to Bishop of London, May 28, 1731, Virginia Magazine of History and Biography, XXXII (May, 1924) 322-323; Exec. Jour. Council Col. Va., IV, 288, 462-464.

74. Virginia Gazette (Rind), January 25, 1770; Maryland Gazette, February 8, 1770; JHB 1770-1772, p. 92. In 1752 two Negroes accused of conspiracy were tried in the York County Court. They were found not guilty of this charge, but during the course of the trial, it appeared to the court that one of them, Tom, was guilty of a misdemeanor, for which he had not been charged, whereupon the justices ordered him given twenty-five lashes. (York County Records, Orders and Judgments, 1752-1754, pp. 204-205.)

their consequences than those of colonial days. The
alertness of the eighteenth-century planters and the
loyalty of some slaves prevented serious racial disturb-
ances.

COUNTERFEITING

In 1756, in a letter to English authorities,
Governor Dinwiddie emphasized the great scarcity of coin
in the colony.[75] There were those, however, who were
attempting to alleviate this shortage, albeit through
illegal means. Counterfeiting, while it does not seem
to have been a constant practice, experienced several
active flurries in eighteenth-century Virginia.

Technically, counterfeiting the king's coin
was high treason and punishable by a horrible death and
attainder.[76] One problem present in the colonies making

---

75. Dinwiddie to the Lords of Trade, February 23,
1756, R. A. Brock, ed., The Official Papers of Robert
Dinwiddie, Lieutenant-Governor of the Colony of Virginia,
1751-1758 (Richmond, 1933), II, 341.

76. In 1736 the punishment for high treason was
described: "The Offender shall be drawn upon a Hurdle,
backward, with his Head downward, from the Prison to

the application of the counterfeiting law more difficult,
was that much of the specie in circulation had been issued
by countries other than England. As early as 1645, the
Assembly had passed a statute designating the death penalty for those who counterfeited foreign coin. The more
drastic feature of the punishment for counterfeiting was
removed in 1755 and 1769 when it was classed simply as a
felony without benefit of clergy; in either high treason
or felony the punishment was death, but in the latter
incident, there was no dismemberment. Because tobacco
notes often were used as a medium of exchange, forging
or counterfeiting these notes was made a felony, although benefit of clergy was not removed until 1765. In
1769, those who knowingly passed counterfeit money became
guilty of a felony, without benefit of clergy.[77]

---

the Gallows, and there hang'd, then cut down alive, his
Privy Members cut off, and his Entrails cut out, his Body
quartered, and his Head and Quarters hang'd up: All his
Lands, Goods, and Chattels, are forfeited, and his Blood
corrupted. But in Counterfeiting &c. of Current Coin,
there is no Corruption of Blood, or Loss of Dower." (Webb,
Justice of Peace, pp. 344-345.)

77. Hening, Statutes, I, 308-309, III, 503, IV,
52-53, 219, 265, VI, 529-530, VIII, 107, 347.

In the early part of the eighteenth century there was little difficulty with counterfeiters in Virginia--perhaps because so much trade was conducted with tobacco as the primary medium of exchange. But as more money circulated through the colony, false coiners became more in evidence. In 1704 there was a small disturbance when two indentured servants were found to be engaged in the "Coyning of false money." In 1743, one person received the death penalty for "coining," while two others, convicted in the same session of the General Court (perhaps accessories), "were whip'd at the Cart's Tail, from the Capitol to the Market place...."[78]

The most colorful counterfeiter in colonial Virginia was Lowe Jackson. This twenty-two year old silversmith of Nansemond County engaged in coining, along with his brothers John and James and one Edward Rumney. Sometime around 1749, Lowe Jackson and several others were brought before the Nansemond County Court charged with counterfeiting, but the case was dismissed after examination by the justices, probably through "some

___

78. JHB 1702-1712, pp. 62-63; Pennsylvania Gazette, July 14, 1743.

chicanery of the lawyers." Jackson, however, remained under suspicion.[79]

The case broke when Robert Lyon, a barber of Williamsburg, was taken up for "uttering base doubloons." These coins, when broken in court, were discovered to be plated with gold, while the insides were "found stark nought." Lyon was subjected to what might be termed an eighteenth-century third degree, the painting in vivid terms the dire consequences of counterfeiting and with possibly the promise of a pardon if he confessed. Lyon broke down and implicated Lowe, John and James Jackson, along with Edward Rumney. A warrant was issued and guards stationed at all ferries, but the counterfeiters made their escape. Extradition proceedings were initiated for the return of Rumney, who was discovered in Maryland. At the time Rumney was a living illustration of the fact that crime does not pay--he was in a Maryland prison for debt.[80]

---

79. John Blair to Lewis Burwell, May 20, 1751, and Dinwiddie to ------, May 20, 1752, PRO CO5/1338, Va. Col. Rec. microfilm.

80. Dinwiddie to -----, May 20, 1752, PRO CO5/1338, Va. Col. Rec. microfilm; W. H. Brown and others, eds., The Archives of Maryland (Baltimore, 1883-1919), XLV, 468-488.

John and James Jackson fled northward, where John was eventually apprehended hiding in a hay stack near Philadelphia. He was committed to a Pennsylvania prison for still other crimes. There is no record that James was ever brought to justice. The ringleader, Lowe Jackson, scurried to North Carolina, there shipping aboard a vessel bound for Barbados. A violent wind drove the vessel back into port, and Jackson made his way overland to Charleston, South Carolina. In the meantime, one James Bird of Virginia had been sent to that city on official business. In Charleston he ran into William Dering, a dancing master late of Williamsburg, who told Bird that he had recently talked with Jackson. When Dering questioned Jackson as to his reason for being in South Carolina, the fugitive had sworn that "a damned fellow of a barber had impeached him and he was forced to flee from justice...." Then, continued Dering, this bold counterfeiter had boasted that "he had coined a hundred." Both Bird and Dering went before a magistrate to swear out a warrant, and Jackson was committed to the local gaol.[81]

---

81. Pennsylvania Gazette, January 22, 1751; Virginia Gazette, April 4, 1751; John Blair to Lewis Burwell, May 20,

Bird returned to Williamsburg to claim the £50 reward offered for the apprehension of Jackson. Edmund Ruffin, "a stout bold man," was employed to return the counterfeiter to Virginia, a journey which cost the government another £100, one-half of which was Ruffin's fee. Ruffin arrived in Williamsburg with his prisoner just before the December court of oyer and terminer. Time was too short to allow the attorney-general to prepare a case, and the prisoner was bound over to the April court. Jackson was ill, so ill that his friends claimed that he was not likely to survive if he was confined in a cold gaol cell without a fire all winter. The gaoler was prevailed upon to allow the prisoner the use of the debtor's cell where Jackson "recruited bravely."[82]

Rain fell steadily on Tuesday, April 16, 1751; nevertheless the courtroom was crowded for the trial of Lowe Jackson. The barber, Robert Lyon, was the chief witness for the prosecution, and he delivered his testimony "with the air and marks of sincerity." Jackson's

---

1751, PRO CO5/1338, Va. Col. Rec. microfilm.

82. Exec. Jour. Council Col. Va., V, 337; John Blair to Lewis Burwell, May 20, 1751, PRO CO5/1338, Va. Col. Rec. microfilm.

attorney tried to discredit Lyon's testimony as "a bid to save his own neck," but was unsuccessful. Between six and seven o'clock that evening, Lowe Jackson was found guilty of counterfeiting.[83]

The friends and counsel of Jackson, though unsuccessful, were at least persistent. After the trial they attempted to prove that several of the grand jury were under age, that another was not a freeholder, and that one of the petit jury was a Quaker. All efforts failed. It also seems that Christopher Jackson, brother of Lowe, tried to intimidate one of the jurors after the trial. John Blair had presided at the trial because of the illness of Lewis Burwell, President of the Council. When Blair received a visit from the father of the convicted man, he displayed proper sympathy, but told the father that he was convinced of the guilt of the son. "I had the public interest to check my private tenderness," he explained. Even as late as May 27, there were rumors that Jackson was to be granted

---

83. "Diary of John Blair," William and Mary Quarterly, 1st series, VII (January, 1899), 137; Virginia Gazette, April 18, 1751.

a new trial because of some technicality.[84]

On May 6, 1751, Lowe Jackson was brought to the bar of the General Court to hear the sentence of death pronounced upon him. His lawyers had submitted an appeal for the king's pardon, four days after the jury's verdict, and had been admitted by the Council by a vote of four to three. The question of a reprieve divided the Council. Jackson himself wrote several letters soliciting the mercy of Council members. And despite his appearance at church in irons, his behavior in prison was anything but pious. He reportedly made threats against John Blair, an act which did little to gain favor with his judges. On the other hand, the condemned man had a powerful friend in Lewis Burwell, President of the Council, who was acting as governor until the arrival of Robert Dinwiddie. On July 31, when the Council met in Gloucester, probably at the home of the ailing president, Blair made a motion about the Jackson case. Burwell stopped him with a curt "desire to hear nothing of it."[85]

---

84. John Blair to Lewis Burwell, May 20, 1751, PRO CO5/1338, Va. Col. Rec. microfilm; "Diary of John Blair," William and Mary Quarterly, 1st series, VII (January, 1899), 139.

85. Virginia Gazette, August 8, 1751; "Diary of

Burwell's influence with the remaining members
of the Council was reflected in the rumor that Blair was
the only one of the group who opposed a reprieve. On
August 8, 1751, the Virginia Gazette noted that the condemned counterfeiter had been granted a reprieve or stay
of execution "'til His Majesty's Pleasure be known." A
little more than a week later, Burwell wrote a most
appealing letter to England favoring a pardon. He made
much of Jackson's youth, asserting at an early age the
accused "was Seduced by one Rumney an infamous Villain...."
He also indicated that another letter, contrary to his
own sentiments, would be arriving from Blair. Blair,
according to Burwell, felt "the poor Creature was unworthy the least Compassion, [and] Tenderness...." The
reports that Jackson had made threats on the life of
Blair were dismissed as fabrications of "a very Drunken
worthless Woman, the Jailor's Wife...."[86]

The following year when Governor Dinwiddie
arrived in Virginia, Lowe Jackson was still languishing

John Blair," William and Mary Quarterly, 1st series, VIII
(July, 1899), 1-17 passim.

86. Lewis Burwell to Dinwiddie, August 17, 1751,
PRO CO5/1338, Va. Col. Rec. microfilm; Virginia Gazette,
August 8, 1751.

in gaol. Dinwiddie had been ordered by his superiors in
England to make a thorough investigation of the Jackson
case. In his report, it was Dinwiddie's impression that
Burwell was "misinformed" as to the true facts of the
case, that the people of "the Country was irritated for
the many impositions of false Money dispersed through
the Colony...," and that Jackson's flight from justice
had been "a tacit acknowledgement of Guilt...." The
trial, he found, had been "conducted with much Candor
and Impartiality." Dinwiddie summed up his findings with
the following observation:

> The Voice of the People is loud against
> him and say if he does not Suffer they can have
> no Security for the Future, and that an Example
> of Justice for so Heinous an Offence is due to
> the offended Country, where ther is still large
> Quantities of false Coin now Current imposed
> upon them.[87]

Whether because of the voice of the people, or
Dinwiddie's report, Jackson's appeal was lost. On March 30,
1753, it was announced that the counterfeiter was "at
length ordered for Execution." On April 13, 1753, just
three days short of two years since his original conviction,

---

87. Dinwiddie to "Right Honourable," May 20, 1752,
PRO CO5/1338, Va. Col. Rec. microfilm.

Lowe Jackson, attended by a minister, was brought from
the public gaol in Williamsburg. Rather than the customary cart, he was drawn to the gallows on a "sledge,"
possibly in lieu of the hurdle specified in executions
for treason. Standing beneath the gallows he addressed
the spectators with "a very moving and pathetic Speech
on the fatal consequences attending an early Habit of
Vice, which had been the Means of bringing him to that
shameful and Untimely End." He demonstrated an unusual
"Composure of Mind," and it was noticed that he died "in
a very penitent Manner." His corpse placed in a coffin
bearing the inscription, "Mercy! triumph over Justice,"
was claimed by his friends for burial in Nansemond
County.[88]

---

88. Maryland Gazette, April 12, May 17, 1753;
Pennsylvania Gazette, May 17, 1753. Jackson was not so
forthright in his dying speech as was one Gilbert Belcher,
who was condemned by the New York authorities for counterfeiting. Before he was turned off, Belcher said that
"no gain afforded me so much pleasure as that which I
acquired by illicit means." (Kenneth Scott, "Colonial
Silversmiths vs. Counterfeiters," Antiques, LXVII [Jan-
uary, 1955], 55. A hurdle was a kind of frame or
sledge on which condemned criminals were drawn from
the prison to the place of execution. In England,
the hurdle remained a part of the punishment for high
treason until 1870.

The Jackson episode appears to have been but one part of an outbreak of counterfeiting along the eastern seaboard. During this same period, Philadelphia was plagued by three gangs of coiners plying their illegal trade in that city. In 1752 North Carolina hanged a group of four counterfeiters, the leader of whom being one Patrick Moore, a tailor from Virginia. And in their confession they implicated Richard Booker of Gloucester County, Virginia, as an accomplice.[89]

The death of Lowe Jackson did not put an end to counterfeiting in Virginia. In fact, in 1758 William Ball, a Burgess from Lancaster County, was expelled from the House for "uttering forged and counterfeit Treasury Notes, Knowing them to be so." By 1764, criminal engravers and printers had played such havoc with the paper currency of the colony that after noting the execution of two criminals for that crime, the Gazette was led to comment:

> The counterfeiting and passing our
> Paper Currency being attended with the
> most destructive Consequences to the Credit
> of the Colony, and large Quantities of it
> being at this Time in Circulation, It is
> to be hoped that all concerned in this base

---

89. Virginia Gazette, May 2, 1751, October 12, November 10, 1752.

and baneful Traffick will take Warning from
the untimely End of those who have now suffered.[90]

The same period also saw a flood of counterfeit
paper currency of Maryland, which was passed as genuine
throughout Virginia. These "ill executed" notes were
the work of William Depriest, head of a group of coiners
in Maryland who was apprehended in the summer of 1767.
It was reported that Depriest had struck off at least
£80,000 in Maryland currency before he was taken up, and
that one of his "Gentlemen of eminent ability" was operating in Virginia. It was during this period that the
Assemblies of both Maryland and North Carolina passed
additional statutes prohibiting the counterfeiting of
Virginia paper money.[91]

The last great currency conspiracy in the Colony of Virginia occurred in the 1770's. There had been
an emission of Treasury Notes provided for by the Assembly

---

90. JHB 1758-1761, p. 50; Virginia Gazette, June 7,
1764.

91. Maryland Gazette, September 17, September 24,
November 19, 1767; Maryland Archives, XXXII, 215-218, LV,
692-693; Virginia Gazette, October 22, December 17, 1767;
York County Records, Judgments, 1759-1763, p. 255; W. L.
Saunders, ed., The Colonial Records of North Carolina
(Raleigh, 1886-1890), VI, 1306.

in 1767, required to be engraved and printed in a fashion
that would "be most safe from counterfeits and forgeries...." The Treasurer of Virginia, Robert C. Nicholas,
designed notes that he thought difficult to reproduce,
yet was not so clever as he thought. The paper currency
provided for under this act was issued in 1771, and almost immediately the counterfeiters were putting out
their own versions. One of them, Samuel Whitworth, was
apprehended before he could establish himself in the
business and charged with "attempting to seduce" two of
William Rind's workers into stealing type, ink, etc.,
from the Gazette office.[92]

By early 1773 there was such a volume of counterfeit money in circulation throughout the colony that
the false notes "put a stop to all Business...," and
trade disrupted. Some thought the actual printing had
been done in Holland, because the spurious notes were
"so exquisitly done, that they have deceived the most
penetrating Geniuses amongst us...." Only through a
careful examination could minute imperfections be

---

92. Hening, Statutes, VIII, 346; Virginia Gazette
(Purdie & Dixon), April 25, September 5, 1771.

discovered. So carefully done were these bills that even the watermarks had been duplicated.[93]

When the passage of false money became so frequent that "the Credit of the Country...[was] deeply affected by it," Governor Dunmore called an emergency meeting of the Council. They, in turn, suggested that a special session of the Assembly be convened. Under the leadership of Richard Henry Lee and Archibald Cary, a bill was passed into law, recalling the currency of 1771 and providing for a new issue that would be more difficult to copy. As a deterrent, there was a re-statement of the severe penalty for counterfeiting. In a sense, this special session of the Assembly re-acted against Governor Dunmore, for out of this meet-ing came the establishment of a permanent Committee of

---

93. Virginia Gazette (Purdie & Dixon), February 11, April 8, 1773; JHB, 1773-1776, pp.viii-ix; Thomas Adams to Perkins, Buchanan and Brown, February 1, 1773, "Letters of Thomas Adams," Virginia Magazine of History and Biography, XXIII (January, 1915), 62; Robert Carter Nicholas to John Norton and Sons, February 12, 1773, Frances Norton Brown, ed., John Norton and Sons, Merchants of London and Virginia, Being the Papers from their Counting House for the Years 1750 to 1795 (Richmond, 1937), p. 302.

Correspondence which was to play such a significant role in the revolutionary crisis.[94]

Copies of this latest act against counterfeiting were dispatched to other colonies, with many following Virginia's lead in making the penalty for the crime more severe. Treasurer Nicholas sent to London for paper "of an exquisite fine Texture," containing water marks that would be difficult to duplicate. The new emission was not absolutely immune from the engraving tools of the counterfeiter, but Nicholas did declare, "that it is much more secure against Counterfeits and Forgeries, than any we have ever had...."[95]

Meanwhile, during all of these legislative machinations, those responsible for all of the confusion had been apprehended, though not until after a number of innocent people had been accused. One John Short, a

---

94. Virginia Gazette (Purdie & Dixon), February 4, March 4, March 18, 1773; Hening, Statutes, VIII, 651-652; JHB 1773-1776, pp. 7-49 passim; Cal. Va. St. Papers, VIII, 2, 5, 16.

95. JHB 1773-1776, pp. 50-62 passim; Robert Carter Nicholas to John Norton and Sons, March 17, 1773, Brown, ed., John Norton and Sons, pp. 305-307; Virginia Gazette (Purdie & Dixon), September 30, 1773.

counterfeiter himself, informed against a ring of fifteen or sixteen counterfeiters, "some of them people of fortune and credit in the country," operating in Pittsylvania County.[96]

After consultation with legal advisors, Dunmore issued a commission to Captain John Lightfoot to capture these criminals. With the assistance of the twenty-five men under his command, Lightfoot found Benjamin Cooke, Joseph Cooke, James Cooke, Benjamin Woodward and Peter Medley working in the shop in Pittsylvania County. Their tools, rolling press, dies for coins, and a large amount of counterfeit currency were taken at the same time. The prisoners were brought to Williamsburg in irons, under a strong guard. Alleged accomplices in other counties were arrested and clapped into local gaols. Some members of the gang fled, followed by Dunmore's proclamation offering a large reward for their capture. An express to the governor of North Carolina, informed him of the existence in that province of "a Nest of the same Pernicious Crew to Society...." A short time later, one Moses Terry was

---

96. Dunmore to Dartmouth, March 13, 1773, PRO CO5/ 1351, Va. Col. Rec. microfilm.

brought in from Halifax County in irons, guarded by the sheriff and nine others. Terry, after his arraignment for counterfeiting, talked as though his life depended upon it--as indeed it may have. He implicated many others, including Paschal Greenhil, a Burgess from Prince Edward County, who managed to clear himself only after numerous depositions testifying to his innocence were printed in the Gazette.[97]

In the arrest of the counterfeiters from Pittsylvania County, Dunmore did not follow customary legal procedures. Because of his fear that a local examining court might release them, he first had them brought to Williamsburg, where they underwent an exam-ination by the governor, the attorney-general and others. So that examining court records might be entered into the proceedings, the accused were sent to Yorktown, where the York County Court remanded them to the General Court. Back in Williamsburg, the counsel for the defense had his clients brought before the General Court on a writ of habeas corpus, attempting to have the case thrown out

---

97. Ibid.; JHB 1773-1776, pp. 12-14, 20, 23-24, 27; Virginia Gazette (Purdie & Dixon) February 25, March 4, April 8, 1773.

because of the illegal procedures used in bringing them to trial. This provoked a "very full and learned Debate," with the final decision finding a majority of the judges declaring the proceedings to be in order and the attorney-general ordered to prepare a bill of indictment.[98]

Despite the mass of evidence against the accused, they were acquitted by the jury. In a clever maneuver the defense counsel, by bringing in sundry witnesses, proved that John Short, chief witness for the prosecution, was "a most atrocious Villain," and went so far as to make a motion that Terry be indicted for perjury. Short fled, leaving behind "a wife and six helpless children, in most pitiable circumstances." The loose-tongued Moses Terry, who had entered a plea of guilty, was granted a pardon by the governor.[99]

There were several others who were charged with counterfeiting within the next few months, but they won their freedom in court. This seems to be, especially in

98. Dunmore to Dartmouth, March 13, 1775, PRO CO5/ 1351, Va. Col. Rec. microfilm; Virginia Gazette (Purdie & Dixon), February 25, March 4, April 15, 1773.

99. Virginia Gazette (Purdie & Dixon), April 22, October 21, 1773.

the days before the outbreak of the Revolution, the general pattern of those tried for counterfeiting; a rather
large number were brought before the General Court, but
there were few convictions. By far the greater number
of the accused were freed than met their death on the
local gallows.

FORGERY

Forgery was defined as "an Offence...where any
person fraudulently makes and publishes false Writings
to the Prejudice of another's Right." Forgeries varied
in degrees of seriousness, the most grave being the forging of deeds, sealed writings, court records and wills.
Under English common law the offender was required to pay
double damages to the injured party, to stand in the
pillory, his ears cut off, his nostrils slit and seared
with a hot iron, forfeit the profits from his lands and
suffer life imprisonment. The second offence demanded
the death sentence. By Virginia statute, all those who
forged tobacco notes, receipts or lottery tickets could
be punished as a felon. A person convicted of any felony

was prohibited from ever holding thereafter any public office, even if later pardoned.[100]

The punishment lessened with the decrease in the frequency of the crime. One of the most frequent instances of forgery was first noted in 1643 when runaway servants began to use forged passes to facilitate their escape. By 1705 the punishment for those persons who forged passes for runaways was a £10 fine and thirty-nine lashes at the whipping post. The lowest form of forgery was that of an "inferiour Nature, as private Letters and such like...." This was not properly considered forgery, and offenders were termed "Cheats" and tried for a misdemeanor rather than a felony, and in the county courts rather than the General Court.[101]

The greatest forgery problem in eighteenth-century Virginia continued to be forged passes used by runaway slaves and indentured servants. Many owners advertising in the Gazette assumed that their fleeing

---

100. Webb, Justice of Peace, p. 163; Starke, Justice of Peace, p. 177; Hening, Statutes, III, 250, IV, 265-266, VI, 460, VIII, 107.

101. Hening, Statutes, I, 254, III, 455, V, 552, VI, 46.

property were possessed of forged papers. The drawing
up of false tobacco notes was equally troublesome, and
the government paid all expenses incurred in the apprehension of such offenders, even if the pursuit carried
the arresting officer across the border into other
colonies.[102]

Indictments for forgery in the General Court,
while not common, were not infrequent. Punishments for
those convicted varied, and there were few acquittals.
In 1739, Samuel MacHenly of King George County was burnt
in the hand, although the year before a person convicted
of forgery had been sentenced to stand in the pillory
for an hour. The forger from Nansemond County, Miles
Mansfield, felt the lashes of the whip, but Hamill Moore
of Essex saw his indictment changed to "Cheat," although
his sentence was an hour in the pillory with a placard
marked "FORGERY" affixed to his chest. Richard Brack of
James City County received the most stringent penalty of
any forger tried before the General Court. In October,

---

102. Virginia Gazette, September 17, 1736, July 14,
1738, April 10, 1752, (Rind) August 25, 1768; Exec. Jour.
Council Col. Va., IV, 351.

1774, Brack was pilloried for one hour. Then, on the second Tuesday in December, his right ear was cut off, after which he suffered a year's imprisonment. Brack's crime, as suggested by his prolonged punishment, was the "forging a Lease, Annuity, Obligation, Bill, Acquittance Relate, or other Discharge of a Personal Matter."[103]

By contrast with other crimes, forgery, other than tobacco notes and certificates used by runaways, was practiced relatively little in colonial Virginia. One interesting conclusion could be that the absence of forgery was a result of the lack of public education and the inability of the criminally inclined to write.

MAIMING (MAYHEM)

The Marquis of Queensbury did not sponsor rules for gentlemanly and sportsmanlike fisticuffs until the nineteenth century, and the word "referee" was unknown in

---

103. Webb, Justice of Peace, pp. 163-164; Virginia Gazette, October 20, 1738, November 2, 1739, April 10, 1752, (Purdie & Dixon) October 17, 1771, October 20, 1774, (Pinkney) June 15, 1775. Henry Marshal, who won acquittal in the General Court, was then ordered to be sent to Hillsboro, North Carolina, because he was suspected of "malpractices" there.

colonial disputes. The "meaner element" fought in a rough and tumble style that could under no circumstances be termed as either genteel or healthy exercise. They were "little restrained by any laws," and the more belligerent kept their nails on the thumb and second finger long, pointed, and hardened over the flame of a candle, the better to pluck out an eye.[104]

It was not until 1752 that the Assembly got around to legal restraints in an effort to curb the boisterous instincts of Virginia's more quick-tempered inhabitants. This statute stated that any person who purposely cut out the tongue, slit the nose, bit or cut off a nose or lip, and cut off or disabled any limb of another was guilty of a felony. Benefit of clergy, however, was allowed for this crime, and the convicted person suffered no corruption of blood or forfeiture. The only three cases brought before the General Court under this law (two for maiming, one for gouging), resulted in convictions, but all three were allowed their clergy

---

104. Thomas Anburey, Travels Through the Interior Parts of America (London, 1789), II, 201-202.

and suffered only the sting of the branding iron.[105]

The injured party was allowed some redress for his disfigurement. A statute, effective in June, 1772, stated that any person who should "wound, by gouging, plucking or putting out an eye, biting, kicking, or stamping upon any of his majesty's subjects" was liable for all damages a jury might assess for the plaintiff, and if he did not pay within three months, he could receive up to thirty-nine lashes at the public whipping post.[106]

The loss of an ear was a serious thing in colonial Virginia--it was the mark of a convicted forger or hog thief. So serious was this injury felt to be, that in 1771 Governor Dunmore offered a £10 reward for the apprehension of Daniel Mackey, who had bitten off the ear of Benjamin Clark of Lunenburg County. In Botetourt County that same year, Charles Given came into the county court requesting a certificate to the effect that his ear had been lost in a fight with Francis

---

105. Hening, Statutes, VI, 250; Virginia Gazette (Purdie & Dixon), November 8, 1770, November 7, 1771, May 9, 1772.

106. Hening, Statutes, VIII, 520-522.

McDonald rather than sliced off as the penalty for hog-stealing.[107]

They played rough in the eighteenth century!

MISDEMEANORS

In most instances, misdemeanors were tried before the county courts, but cases of "Transcendent Malignity: Such are a Complication of divers Crimes, tending to the Universal Prejudice of the Subject, or the total Subversion of the Government in Church and State," fell within the jurisdiction of the General Court. This was a flexible definition, and it is most frustrating to attempt to determine just what did constitute a misdemeanor serious enough to be tried before the highest court. Misdemeanors in the colony were defined under English common law, and it seems that the responsibility for determining the court for trial rested with the examining court. Crimes classed as serious misdemeanors included: challenging another to a duel; exposing a naked

---

107. Virginia Gazette (Rind), November 21, 1771; Oren Frederic Morton, A History of Rockbridge County, Virginia (Staunton, 1920), p. 59.

person in a public place; seducing an apprentice in a

bawdy house and forcing him to spend his master's money;

an expression of the intent to kill a person; reading a

paper falsely to an illiterate person; storing a large

amount of gunpowder too near a church or another house;

using crooked dice; buying and selling goods known to be

stolen; and cheating at cards, dice, or any other game

of chance.[108]

At least ten persons were tried before the

General Court between 1766 and 1773 under an indictment

listed simply as a "Misdemeanor." Five of these were

women, and only two out of the ten were acquitted. Pun-

ishments included fines ranging from forty shillings to

£20, in addition to imprisonment from one to twelve

months. The only two misdemeanors explained in the

records were in 1751 when John Sparks was found guilty

of an attempted highway robbery and the following year

when John Boak was convicted for receiving stolen tobacco.[109]

---

108. Webb, Justice of Peace, p. 230; Starke, Justice
of Peace, pp. 266-267.

109. Virginia Gazette (Purdie & Dixon),April 18,
1751, April 18, June 13, 1766, December 10, October 22,
1767, October 17, 1771, December 16, October 21, 1773;
Pennsylvania Journal or Weekly Advertiser, July 26, 1750;

In most cases it seems that these were
aggravated instances of lesser crimes where the penalty
involved a fine of more than twenty shillings.[110] Even
then a misdemeanor trial was a rarity in the General
Court, for cases of this nature seldom got past the
county court.

MURDER

"Murder is, the Killing any Person, within the
Realm, upon Malice forethought, the Death ensuing within
a Year and a Day after the Stroke given." Unintentional
murder, without malice, or accidental killing, was changed
in the designation to manslaughter.[111]

The penalty for willful murder was death without benefit of clergy, and this--along with treason--was
a felony that could not be pardoned by the governor. On
the other hand, there were varying degrees of homicide,

Hening, Statutes, V, 524-525.

110. Webb, Justice of Peace, pp. 232-233.

111. Starke, Justice of Peace, pp. 194-201.

some of which lessened the charge to manslaughter, which
was clergyable. Among these were justifiable homicide,
homicide by misadventure, or homicide in self-defense.
The charge of murder was, of course, dependent upon the
presence of premeditation. There was also one other
classification under the general heading of murder or
homicide; Felo de se, committed by "a Person who, being
of sound Mind, and of the Age of Discretion, voluntarily
killeth himself." In addition to the death sentence for
willful murder, there was corruption of blood, forfeiture
of goods, chattels and fee-simple lands. Those convicted
on the lesser charge of manslaughter were branded on the
brawn of the left thumb with the letter M, and they
suffered no corruption of blood or loss of property. A
suicide, or one who had committed self-murder, was not
allowed a Christian burial, his goods and chattels were
forfeit, but his lands were retained by his survivors.[112]

The results of fifty-nine murder trials reported
in the Virginia Gazette offer some interesting statistics.
Of this number, thirty-two received the death sentence,
while twenty-five were acquitted. Two had their original

---

112. Webb, Justice of Peace, pp. 236-238.

indictments for murder changed to manslaughter. Included
among those tried for murder were twelve women, accused
of murdering their bastard children. The results of
these trials suggest that colonial justice sometimes
deviated into strange paths, even after acquittal. The
obstreperous Robert Cooke of Henrico, for instance, won
his acquittal on a murder charge, but was returned to
jail and forced to remain there until he could furnish
security for his good behavior. Nathan Phillips of
Hanover was also placed behind bars after being declared
not guilty, but the reason given was because of his
"being a lunatick."[113]

There were a number of white men tried for
killing Negro slaves. In 1739, Charles Quin, an overseer in Essex County, and his accessory before the fact,
David White, were convicted of whipping a slave to death
"in a most cruel and barbarous manner." Both were hanged.
Andrew Bourne (or Byrn), another overseer, had been convicted ten years earlier of a similar crime by a jury in
the General Court. The judges who sat on his trial felt

---

113. Virginia Gazette (Purdie & Dixon), December 10,
1772, June 10, 1773.

the verdict unjust, and they petitioned the Governor in

Council to reprieve the overseer and request a pardon

from the king. The evidence brought out in the trial

indicated that the slave had been an habitual runaway;

Bourne had been so "transported with anger" when the

slave was caught that he had given him an "immoderate

correction," and the Negro had died. Governor Gooch

felt that the execution of the overseer would set an

unhappy precedent and give slaves an occasion for inso-

lence which they had not demonstrated before, and inter-

ceded on Bourne's behalf to the king.[114]

There were other occasions when the governor

interceded for persons condemned for murder, especially

when he felt that there had been a miscarriage of justice.

Upon one such occasion, a servant was cleared by the con-

fession of his alleged accomplice, but a pardon was still

required from the king once a person had been convicted.

In other instances the jury brought in a verdict of

murder when the judges felt that the charge should have

---

114. Ibid., November 3, November 24, 1739; Gooch to
"Your Grace," June, 1729, PRO CO5/1337, Va. Col. Rec. microfilm; Exec. Jour. Council Col. Va., IV, 206.

been lowered to manslaughter.[115]

Because of the eccentricities of the human mind, the manner in which crimes were discovered took many forms; in one instance the supernatural even played a part in the solution of a murder. William Marr, along with three other runaway servants, murdered Liselet Larby, a professional hunter of Orange County who they had been afraid would report their whereabouts. Marr's companions fled, but he had a troublesome conscience. He was finally driven to a confession because of the continued "Apparition of the murder'd Man's tormenting him." When two of his companions were captured in Pennsylvania, they were returned to Virginia and upon Marr's testimony found guilty of murder.[116]

The most famous murder case in colonial Virginia was never brought to trial. The crime occurred June 3, 1766, in Benjamin Mosby's tavern at Cumberland Courthouse. Robert Routlidge of Prince Edward County,

---

115. Dinwiddie to "Right Honourable," July 20, 1752, PRO CO5/1338; and Fauquier to the Board of Trade, August 1, 1765, PRO CO5/1345, Va. Col. Rec. microfilm.

116. Virginia Gazette, June 10, October 21, 1737.

a Scottish merchant and "a worthy blunt man, of strict
honesty and sincerity, a man incapable of fraud and
hypocrisy," was joined by a group of local men, including Colonel John Chiswell. Chiswell had been drinking,
and was talking in a loud voice "and somewhat liberal
of oaths." His friend Routlidge rebuked him for his
profaneness, whereupon Chiswell turned upon the merchant, accusing him of being "a fugitive rebel, a villain who came to Virginia to cheat and defraud men of
their property, and a Presbyterian fellow...." This
was more than Routlidge could take, and in his anger
threw a glass of wine in Chiswell's face. The Colonel
successively tried to throw a bowl of toddy, a candle-
stick, and a pair of tongs at the merchant, but was
restrained by other members of the party. A servant
was sent for Chiswell's sword. With his weapon in his
hand, Chiswell ordered Routlidge out of the room, asserting him "unworthy to appear in such company." The
"hickuping" merchant refused to leave, and while a room
was being unlocked to put him in, he was subjected to
much abuse by Chiswell, who repeatedly referred to him
as a "Presbyterian fellow." Chiswell, refusing to allow

his sword to be taken from him, stalked across the room,
leaned across a table and ran Routlidge through the heart.
The Colonel then calmly handed his weapon to his servant,
called for a bowl of toddy, and continued his abuse of
the dead man, saying "He deserves his fate, damn him; I
aimed at his heart, and I have hit it." By the time a
justice arrived to hold a preliminary hearing, the Colonel
was quite drunk.[117]

Chiswell was committed to the county prison without bail. In the ensuing days he demonstrated no remorse,
and told a number of conflicting stories as to the manner
in which Routlidge met his death. The examining court
ordered him taken to Williamsburg to the public gaol.
Upon his arrival in the capital, three members of the
Council, John Blair, William Byrd III and Presley Thompson,
stopped the sheriff and his prisoner, held a brief examining court of their own, and admitted the Colonel to
bail. Such arbitrary action raised a storm of criticism,
throwing "the whole country into ferment," with many
feeling this to be a form of discrimination in favor of
the gentry. John Blair attempted to answer criticism

---

117. Ibid., (Purdie & Dixon), July 18, 1766.

with a feeble recitation of the details of the case,
with the _Gazette_ offering strong rebuttal. George Wythe,
who had been consulted by the Councillors as to the
legality of their action, felt constrained to publish
his reasons for suggesting that the admittance of bail
to Chiswell was legal. His argument was that since the
King's Bench, the highest court in England, held that
right, it only followed that the General Court, the
highest court in Virginia, retained that same authority.
New accusations followed explanations, in turn calling
for additional explanation. Witnesses, when their
veracity was questioned, angrily defended their integrity
in the local press. Colonel Chiswell, perhaps unwillingly,
settled the issue. In October, 1766, at his home in
Williamsburg, he suddenly died of "nervous fits, owing
to a constant uneasiness of the mind." The controversy,
however, lingered on through several issues of the _Gazette_,
with both sides attempting to get in the last word.[118]

---

118. _Ibid._, June 20, July 4, July 11, July 25,
August 1, September 12, September 19, October 10, October 17, October 30, 1766; Rev. John Camm to Mrs. Walter
McClurg, July 24, 1766, _William and Mary Quarterly_, 1st
series, II (April, 1894), 238-239.

Other murder trials that never reached the General Court were those of slaves, who were tried in county courts of oyer and terminer under a commission issued by the governor. Because the murder of a master or mistress by a slave was considered petit treason, punishments meted out by the county courts often varied from those of the General Court. A Negro slave who confessed to the murder of her mistress in Nansemond County was burned to death in 1737. A Negro male slave, after having received "pretty severe Correction," killed his master, his mistress, and their three children, and then decapitated the bodies before making his escape. After his capture, the Surry County Court ordered him hanged immediately after the trial, his head to be then cut off and his body burned.[119]

There was, upon at least one occasion, a murder case that fell without the jurisdiction of any Virginia court. In 1770, David Ferguson, master of the Virginia ship, Betsy, was lodged in the public gaol, charged with the murder of a Negro boy and three mariners under his command. The judges of the General Court felt that they held no jurisdiction over a crime committed on

---

119. Virginia Gazette, February 25, 1737; Maryland Gazette, February 7, 1754.

the high seas, although other colonial courts had used

an English statute designed to suppress piracy for

similar trials. Governor Botetourt and his Council did

not feel that this was the proper procedure, although

they could try him for the death of the Negro boy,

Caesar, Ferguson's slave and whose death had occurred

within the Virginia capes. Captain Ferguson was acquitted

of Caesar's death, but was ordered back to prison until

a decision could be reached in London as to the final

disposition of the case. In England, the king's attorney-

general ruled that if Ferguson was acquitted in his trial

in Virginia for the death of Caesar, he should be returned

to England to be tried for the murder of the three mariners

whom he reputedly killed "in a cruel and undeserved manner."

Ferguson was accordingly sent to England in the custody

of a Captain Walker. In London he was examined by the

lord mayor, who committed him to prison to await trial

before the next session of the admiralty court. Although

Ferguson had been acquitted of his slave's murder in

Virginia, he seems to have been placed in double jeopardy,

for it was reported that he was tried once again for

"the Murder of his Cabin Boy...." On January 4, 1771,

David Ferguson paid the supreme penalty for murder upon
the gallows at Execution Dock in London.[120]

The gallows were sometimes cheated if the jury
changed an indictment from murder to manslaughter. Although manslaughter was a clergyable crime, three men
from Pittsylvania County in 1774 were not granted their
freedom, but were sent back to prison to await transportation to Salisbury in North Carolina, "being guilty of
some notorious offences" in that place. In some instances the governor issued a pardon for manslaughter,
sparing the convicted person the indignity of the brand
on his left thumb. This was the case on at least one
occasion when the convicted man had been adjudged se
defendo, or of having killed in self defence.[121]

The governor, at times, also granted clemency
in cases where the guilty person had laid "violent hands

120. John Randolph to Botetourt, June 26, 1770,
Hillsborough to Attorney-General, March 31, 1770,
Attorney-General to Hillsborough, April 5, 1770, Botetourt
to Mr. Conway, July 31, 1770, PRO CO5/1348, Va. Col. Rec.
microfilm; Virginia Gazette (Rind), January 25, April 19,
1770, February 7, 1771; Maryland Gazette, February 8, 1770,
April 4, 1771.

121. Virginia Gazette, December 4, 1739, (Purdie &
Dixon) April 18, 1771, November 4, 1773, October 20,
1774; Exec. Jour. Council Col. Va., II, 288, IV, 31.

upon himself," and had been judged a suicide. When the forfeiture of the possessions of the deceased constituted a hardship upon his survivors, the governor could grant a remission of the forfeit if the value was not above £10. If they were valued above that amount, it was not unknown that the governor forward an appeal to the king for re-mission.[122]

Ever since Cain and Abel, violent death has been listed amongst the frailties of man. The Virginians had their share of murders among them, and their only recourse in the way of a deterrent was an appeal to Mosaic law.

PERJURY

The basic punishment for perjury in colonial Virginia was derived from English statute law; a person convicted of perjury was required to pay a forfeit of £20 in addition to a six months imprisonment. If he had no property whose value would amount to this sum, he was forced to stand in the pillory with his ears nailed to

---

122. Exec. Jour. Council Col. Va., III, 138; Gooch to "Your Grace," July 29, 1730, PRO CO5/1337, Va. Col. Rec. microfilm.

it. Furthermore, he was disabled as a witness in any court of record. The punishment for those convicted of persuading or suborning a witness to commit perjury was a forfeiture of goods to the value of £40. If he owned no property of that value, he was imprisoned six months, stood in the pillory for one hour (ears unnailed), and was disabled as a witness.[123]

Virginians added refinements to meet local conditions. In 1745 the Assembly made the swearing of false oaths identical with "committing wilful and corrupt perjury," and no person convicted of this felony could hold public office in the colony. Later, persons swearing to false tobacco certificates were liable to a fine of 1,000 pounds of tobacco.[124]

In reality, there were more cases of criminal perjury in the seventeenth century than there were in the eighteenth. One of the better known is the case of Edward Sharpless, Clerk of the Council, who gave

---

123. Webb, Justice of Peace, pp. 241-242; Starke, Justice of Peace, pp. 274-275.

124. Hening, Statutes, III, 250, V, 349, 363, 483, IV, 355, 471, VI, 153.

confidential documents to the royal commissioners in
1625. This was considered perjury because Sharpless had
violated his oath of secrecy. He was sentenced to stand
in the pillory and lose his ears.[125]

In the eighteenth century there were occasional
references to perjury in the county courts, but even there
it was a relatively infrequent charge. In 1705, in the
well-known dispute between Governor Nicholson and
Commissary James Blair, the latter was at one time suffering "under ye Scandal of being a Perjured Person."
In later years, in charges to the grand jury, Governor
Dinwiddie sometimes reminded that body that "Perjury in
Judicial Concerns is a dreadful Complicat'n of Guilt,
it's a daring Insult on the Diety, and the most scanda-
lous, as well as dangerous Invasion of the Property of
Others."[126]

---

125. H. R. McIlwaine, ed., Minutes of the Council
and General Court of Colonial Virginia, 1622-1632, 1670-
1671, with notes and Excerpts From Original Council and
General Court Records, into 1683, Now Lost (Richmond,
1924), p. 14.

126. Certain clergymen of Virginia to the Arch-
bishop of Canterbury, June 3, 1705, Virginia Magazine
of History and Biography, VIII (January, 1901) 274;
R. A. Brock, ed., The Official Papers of Robert Dinwiddie,
Lieutenant-Governor of the Colony of Virginia, 1751-1758
(Richmond, 1933), I, 36.

Yet, there are few cases of perjury to be
found among the available General Court records. In
1773, the king's case against the counterfeiting ring
was lost because John Short, the principal witness for
the prosecution, was accused of perjury. The counsel
for the defense went so far in this instance as to make
a motion that he be indicted for perjury. But Short fled,
depriving the records of at least one trial in the higher
courts for perjury. There was no report that he was ever
caught.[127]

PIRACY

Piracy was a capital offence, but the discussion
here is abbreviated because it was not a crime triable
before the General Court, as such. Pirates were tried
before a court of vice-admiralty, appointed by a commission issued under the great seal of England, or the
seal of the admiralty. The jurisdiction of this court
included all piracies, felonies and robberies committed
on the high seas. A court of vice-admiralty was composed

_____

127. Virginia Gazette (Purdie & Dixon), April 22,
1773.

of seven persons, one of whom, the presiding officer, was to be the governor, the lieutenant-governor, or a member of the Council; the remaining six to be selected from among merchants, planters, military or naval officers, or officers serving aboard merchant vessels.

Conviction as a pirate brought loss of life, lands, goods and chattels, but there was no corruption of blood; benefit of clergy was not allowed a convicted pirate, "because it is not an offence punishable at Common Law, but by Civil Law, which does not allow Clergy in any case."[128]

Between 1700 and 1730 the colony of Virginia suffered a plague of pirates. After that latter date, marking the end of the "Golden Age of Piracy," the jolly roger was seldom seen in Virginia waters.

RAPE

Rape was defined as "having unlawful and carnal Knowledge of a Woman by Force and against her Will." The penalty for rape was death, without benefit of clergy.

---

128. Webb, Justice of Peace, pp. 248-250.

Accessories in a rape case were likewise considered felons
and suffered the same penalty as the person accused of
the primary crime. A woman so ravished was required to
register her complaint within forty days, "because Concealing it implies Consent before the Fact." On the
other hand,if consent was obtained through threats of
death, it was still considered rape "because Consent
ought to be free and voluntary." Consent was no factor
in sexual relations with a girl under ten years of age,
for in such instances it was considered statutory rape.[129]

In the extant records there are only eight cases
of rape tried before the General Court during the eighteenth century. Of these, five were acquitted, two were
hanged, while one of those convicted received a pardon
from the governor.[130]

There were a number of slaves tried for this
crime in the county courts of oyer and terminer. In most

---

129. Ibid., pp. 261-263; Starke, Justice of Peace,
pp. 292-293, 353.

130. Virginia Gazette, June 12, 1752, (Purdie &
Dixon) May 7, 1767, October 25, November 8, 1770,
October 21, December 16, 1773, April 21, 1774, October 24,
1775, (Dixon and Hunter) April 22, 1775.

cases the convicted slave was hanged, but upon one occasion, upon a petition by his owner, a Negro received the pardon of the governor.[131]

In some instances, it seems that the county courts felt that castration was the proper punishment for a slave convicted of rape. This punishment was based upon a 1723 statute that allowed the justices of the county courts to order dismemberment in any fashion "not touching life, as the said county shall think fit." Castration became unlawful in 1769, when the court was enjoined from ordering it in the case of any slave, except upon conviction for raping, or attempting to rape, a white woman.[132]

There were some instances when sexual assaults were made upon young girls. An Indian slave was held in the Yorktown prison for such a crime, but unfortunately there are no records of the eventual disposition of the case. In Isle of Wight County, a free Negro attempted to ravish a young white girl of about seven years of age.

131. JHB 1773-1776, pp. 357, 406; Legis. Jour. Council Col. Va., III, 1596.

132. Hening, Statutes, IV, 132, VIII, 358.

He was convicted and sentenced to stand in the pillory
for one hour, during which time he was "much pelted by
the populace." After he was removed, he was "smartly
Whipp'd" by the application of "29 Lashes well laid on
his bare back." Some time after this initial punishment,
he was sold into slavery "for the Payment of his Fees."[133]

Rape was not a prevalent crime in colonial
Virginia. Perhaps it was because of the generally
accepted loose morals among the lower levels of society,
and it did not become a crime until it transcended social
or color barriers.

TREASON

Treason was:

a Crime of such Transcendent Malignity, in
its Nature and Consequences, that it is, by
the Law, distinguished for its Superior
Guilt, and thereby punishable in the most
base and ignominious Manner: Other offences
are injurious to Private Persons only, but
this is a Public Mischief, and often strikes
at the Root of all Civil Government.[134]

---

133. Virginia Gazette, August 26, 1737, October 27,
1738.

134. Webb, Justice of Peace, pp. 342-343.

In the usual acceptance of the word, treason encompassed any rebellion, sedition, or speaking in a derogatory manner of the king or government. There were two kinds, high treason and petit treason. Technically, counterfeiting was considered high treason, as was a rebellion fomented by slaves.

There were several instances of high treason in seventeenth-century Virginia, and among them is one of the most famous in the colony, an insurrection that is sometimes stressed as the first stirrings of liberty in this country. But in 1736, George Webb, writing in his Justice of Peace said:

> The only Instance of Trial and Conviction of Treason hitherto extant upon our Records, is that of Nathaniel Bacon, Junior, and his Accomplices, who were attainted, executed, and their Estates forfeited, for Rebellion, and Trason, A.D. 1676. The Principal Traitor, Bacon, escaped legal Sentence and Execution, by a Natural Death, but was attainted by Act of Assembly, pass'd under the Great Seal of England.[135]

The internal turmoil of a civil insurrection continued as a lingering fear in the colony of Virginia. In 1711, when Colonel Thomas Carey raised the standard

---

135. Ibid., p. 344.

of rebellion in North Carolina, so great was the fear that the insurrection would spread (especially after it was rumored that Virginians were involved), and perhaps lead to a mass exodus of servants and slaves, that the Council of Virginia not only offered to mediate the dispute, but issued a proclamation calling for the apprehension of Carey and other ringleaders should they cross the border.[136]

Petit treason, the customary form in colonial Virginia, could be committed under three conditions: a servant killing his master or mistress; a wife killing her husband; or an "Ecclesiastical Person" murdering his superior. In all of these instances there was the primary question of obediance and allegiance. In effect, petit treason was "no more than Murder in its most odious Degree, except in point of Trial and Punishment."[137]

In punishments for petit treason, male criminals were to be drawn to the place of execution, hanged

---

136. Exec. Jour. Council Col. Va., III, 277, 281; Colonial Records of North Carolina, I, 776-777; Dartmouth to Lords of Trade, September 25, 1711, PRO CO5/1363, Va. Col. Rec. microfilm.

137. Starke, Justice of Peace, p. 346.

and then quartered. Women convicted of petit treason were first strangled into insensibility and then burned.[138]

During the eighteenth century, all recorded cases of petit treason involved slaves. In 1733, the County Court of Goochland ordered the hanging and quartering of the Negroes, Valentine and Champion, for the murder of Robert Allen. After the execution the sheriff submitted his expense account. Among his charges was one item calling for the payment of 2,000 pounds of tobacco "for providing Tarr, burying the trunk, cutting out the quarters, a Pott, Carts & horses, carrying and setting up the heads & quarters of the two Negroes at the places mentioned by order of the Court." Four years later a Negro woman was burned for murdering her mistress in Nansemond County. In 1754, when a slave murdered his master and his entire family, the Surry County Court ordered him hanged, his head placed on a pole, and his body burnt. As late as 1767, four Negroes found guilty of conspiring to poison their overseers were hanged and their heads ordered fixed to the chimneys of the courthouse in Alexandria.[139]

---

138. Webb, Justice of Peace, pp. 345-346.

139. Virginia Magazine of History and Biography, I (January, 1894), 328-330; Virginia Gazette, February 25,

All of the above cases were tried in the county courts. There seems to have been no trials for petit treason in the General Court during the eighteenth century. The only occasion when there might have been such a trial in the higher court was that of a Mrs. Thompson of York, who murdered her husband with an axe as he slept. She was found to be deranged, however, and not brought to trial. Perhaps wives really were obedient and loyal in the eighteenth century.[140]

WITCHCRAFT

By the eighteenth century, the charge of witchcraft seems to have become obsolete in Virginia. In fact, most of the cases in the seventeenth century seem not to have progressed beyond the county courts--if that far. One of the first instances of an accusation of witchcraft in Virginia was made by the Reverend Francis Doughty, who himself had been accused of "many Vices and especially to Drinking." Doughty, pastor of Hungars Parish in Accomac,

---

1737; _Maryland Gazette_, February 7, 1754; _Boston Chronicle_, January 18, 1768.

140. _Virginia Gazette_ (Rind), July 16, 1769.

had been forced out of his vicarship in Old Sodbury,
England, because of his Puritan tendencies. He had come
to Virginia by way of Massachusetts, Rhode Island and New
Netherlands. Sometime before 1659 he had charged Barbara
Winbrow of having lived a wicked life and accused her of
"Witchery." Nothing seems to have come of his charges,
but Doughty, after he moved to Maryland, was to accuse
another woman of witchcraft because she knew how to swim,
but again it was decided there was "no Cause for Action."[141]

There was one well-known case in which Colonel
John Washington, great grandfather of George, was involved. He accused Edward Prescott, merchant and owner
of a merchant ship, of hanging an accused witch, one
Elizabeth Richardson, at sea. When Prescott was tried
in Maryland he was acquitted because Washington refused
to come from his home in Westmoreland County, Virginia,
on the date set for the trial, "Because then god willing
I intend to gett my yowng sonne baptized, All the Company
& Gossips being already invited."[142]

---

141. Philip Alexander Bruce, Institutional History
of Virginia in the Seventeenth Century (New York, 1910),
I, 218.

142. Maryland Archives, III, 306-308; XLI, 327-329.

Perhaps the best known case of Virginia witch-craft was that of Grace Sherwood. Grace, "the Virginia Witch," was accused in Princess Anne County Court and the case sent to the General Court in 1698. The attorney-general felt that there was not enough evidence to find a true bill and the case was sent back to the county to "make a further Enquiry into the Matter." Nothing seems to have been done, for Grace Sherwood apparently lived out her life without further ado, since her will was not probated until 1733.[143]

Had Grace Sherwood been tried before the General Court and been found guilty, she might have suffered a felon's death without benefit of clergy. A lesser charge was petit witchcraft, although there is no evidence that this charge was ever pressed. This involved the use of charms for various purposes--"To provoke Love," for example--and if found guilty the witch was to suffer one year's imprisonment, to stand in the pillory every quarter of that year and there publicly confess her transgressions.[144]

---

143. Exec. Jour. Council Col. Va., III, 78; Lower Norfolk County Virginia Antiquary, III (1901), 55-57.

144. Webb, Justice of Peace, pp. 361-362.

Virginia was coming of legal age in the eighteenth century, and some of the superstitions of the past were being pushed into the background of jurisprudence. Crime and mortal criminals caused enough trouble without calling in the supernatural.

INDEX

Botetourt, Gov., 213
Bourne, Andrew, 112, 206-207
Brack, Richard, 198-199
Branding, See Burning
Brown, Edward, 144n
Browne, William, Col., 12
Brumskill, John, Rev., 43n
Burgard, John, 147
Burgesses, House of, 63, 75n, 101n
Burglary, 148-171; See also Robbery, Stealing
Burning as punishment, 65, 107-108, 198   205
Burwell, Lewis, 183, 184-185
Byrd, William II, church attendance of 64n; on burglary
    in Va., 148; on courts, 30-31, 34, 47-48, 53n, 87n;
    on rape cases, 86; on slaves, 172
Byrd, William, III, 210

Campbell, Christiana, 156
Capital punishment, and charter of 1606, 2; for arson, 133;
    for bastardy, 136, 137; for blasphemy, 143; for
    counterfeiting, 177-178, 179, 187; for felonies, 114-
    122; for murder, 204-206, 212, 214; for piracy, 218-
    219; for rape, 219, 220, 221; for slave insurrections,
    173, 174, 175; for stealing, 149, 153-154, 156, 159,
    162, 164, 166-171; for treason, 224-225; for witch-
    craft, 228; restricted to higher courts, 9, 28, 30,
    45
Capitol, Williamsburg, 17-19, 39, 130-131
Carey, Thomas, Col., 223-224
Carter, Charles, Col., 94n
Carter, Robert, 58n, 134
Cary, Archibald, 191
Castration, 221
Cattle-stealing, 7
Chaplains, 63-64, 86n, 115
Charter, 1606, 2-3; 1609, 3-4; 1612, 4-5
Children, 97
Chiswell, John, Col., 209-211
Church of England, 145
Circumstantial evidence, 100
Civil cases, 2, 22, 45